PEOPLE AT WORK in CHINA

FRANCES WOOD

B.T. BATSFORD LTD   LONDON

CONTENTS

Background to Modern China 3
Agriculture 10
    The rich peasant family 13
    The poor peasant family 15
Industry 18
    The silk-reeling factory worker 20
    The embroidery factory worker 22
    The coalminer 24
The Professions 27
    The lawyer 28
    Two doctors 30
    The teacher 33
Service Industries 36
    The tourist guide 38
    The elderly waiter and his wife 40
    Two self-employed boys 43
Transportation 45
    Boat people 48
    The bus driver 50
    The taxi driver 51
Arts and Crafts 54
    The Hani embroiderer 56
    The young painter 57
Glossary 61
Book List and Acknowledgments 62
Index 63

© Frances Wood 1987

First published 1987

All rights reserved. No part of this publication may be reproduced in any form or by any means without permission from the Publisher.

Typeset by Tek-Art Ltd, Kent
and printed in Great Britain by
R J Acford
Chichester, Sussex
for the publishers
B.T. Batsford Ltd
4 Fitzhardinge Street
London W1H 0AH

ISBN 0 7134 5266 8

Frontispiece
Rush-hour in Peking, dominated by bicycles.

BACKGROUND TO MODERN CHINA

A common image of China is of people at work, in huge numbers. Some rather disparaging writers have described China as a nation of "blue ants", blue referring to the colour of today's working clothes in China (in the past, peasants wore black) and ants obviously implying busy, bustling activity. It is not such a bad image, for the Chinese, for over a thousand years, had been organized by their imperial rulers to undertake huge projects, such as building the Great Wall — the only man-made structure of sufficient size to be recognized from the moon by the first astronauts — and to maintain a system of roads covering their vast country. Recently, after Mao Zedong and the Communist Party took power in 1949, the people have continued to work with their hands, building huge dams, dykes to keep the Yellow River from bursting its banks and canals to irrigate hundreds of square miles of land — all with very little machinery to lighten the work.

Loess, or "yellow earth", covers much of north China. It is fertile but easily eroded and irrigation is difficult on the slopes. North China was almost bare of trees by the beginning of the Ming dynasty (1368), as timber was the main building material as well as a major source of fuel. Terraces have been built to prevent further erosion but there is no sign of the massive tree-planting that can be seen elsewhere in China.

AGRICULTURE

As a country where most people still live by agriculture China is very unmechanized: most work in the fields is still done by hand. In the last ten years, the Communist Party has decided that work should be carried out by families, not by the artificially created "teams" that were used before, and families don't possess many machines: they work small fields where machines would be useless, so the pattern continues.

Naturally, as China covers such a vast area, being the second largest country in the world (second only to the Soviet Union in size), agricultural patterns vary considerably according to the local climate and topography. In the last few decades the weather has been unkind to China. The North has been suffering from drought for more than ten years and water has to be pumped from increasing depths underground. The South, by contrast, has been repeatedly flooded. These problems are not as acute as they were before the Communists took over in 1949, for their priorities included building dykes to prevent the terrible floods that used to drown thousands of people and thousands of acres, and providing the northern farmers with electrical pumps to supply water.

TRANSPORT

Another aspect of modernization has been the improvement in communications, by rail, road and water, so that the produce of the richer, more fertile, South can be more easily transported to the barren North.

Though the first railways in China were built by foreigners in the nineteenth century, since 1949 the Chinese Government has constructed thousands of miles of track. In the last few years a major priority has been road-building, which is cheaper and equally essential. Many of the older country roads are now too narrow for the volume of motor traffic, mostly lorries and public buses, and these are now being widened to avoid accidents and jams.

Southern China is criss-crossed by rivers and canals, and exploitation of these has led to a growth in river transport and also fish-farming on a huge scale. All over south China you can see nets in the lakes, ponds and rivers, often with a public lavatory set up over the water so that the manure adds to the food chain.

Pigs going to market in Sichuan province. The black pig with the squashy nose is a typical Chinese pig; the longer-nosed pink pigs are new types imported to improve breeds.

TOURISM Air transport is also expanding in China. Though there were two rival air companies before 1949, only one remained after the Communist takeover. Air transport is still used mainly for people rather than goods and it has played a major part in the movement of tourists around the country. As a very large proportion of China's foreign exchange is earned from tourism, expanding aviation facilities for foreign tourists is still a major priority. In Xi'an, where the famous terracotta army of the Qin emperor was provided for his tomb 2000 years ago, the numbers of tourists are so great that the airport is being extended to allow for the arrival of jumbo jets. At the same time, all sorts of other tourist facilities, hotels in particular, are being constructed at top speed, providing more ways in which the State can earn foreign currency, which in turn is used to purchase foreign equipment and expertise to speed China's modernization.

INDUSTRY Industrial development in China was badly disrupted by the conservative attitude of the last dynasty (1644-1911), by competition from Japan in the 1930s and by the chaos of revolution. Nevertheless, China is extremely rich in natural resources. The problem has been how to exploit them and this has been complicated by lack of technical expertise and transportation facilities. Though China is self-sufficient, her industries badly need modernization and improvements in efficiency, and though she is a major exporter, particularly of textiles — cotton, silk and cashmere — she has consistently to meet international standards and face competition and trade barriers.

BREAKING WITH THE PAST

Despite China's potential, various factors are still holding her back. One is the importance of the past. China has the world's longest continual civilization, an unbroken tradition going back more than 4000 years, and the habits of millenia are difficult to break. One of these was the traditional subjugation of women.

In traditional China it was not considered proper for women, except those from peasant families, to work. The practice of foot-binding, introduced in the twelfth century, where the toes were bent under the foot and kept tightly bound from the age of six or seven, made women virtually immobile. Though the custom was first banned in 1911, it persisted until 1949, when the Communists took over. They believed firmly in women's equality and have passed many laws protecting women's rights. Nowadays, women do the same work as men and are entitled to equal pay for equal jobs.

In traditional China the rich were those who owned land. The most glorious job was one in the imperial civil service, so the rich educated their sons in order to help them pass the exams which would enable them to become government officials. Merchants were despised, as were soldiers, who were considered to be little more than bandits. If merchants could afford it they would buy land and try to educate their sons to become officials, for that was the way to the top of society. In Communist China, however, intellectuals are held in low esteem: it is the productive labourer, who contributes to the national wealth, who is considered superior.

RELIGION

The three religions of early China had different attitudes to life. Confucianism, based on the ideas of Confucius, a wandering teacher of the fifth century B.C., was the State religion. It started as a philosophy, or code of conduct. Confucius believed that the Emperor ruled with heaven's permission, or "mandate". If all was well and the people were prosperous this was a sign of heaven's approval. If people were starving and there were earthquakes or other natural disasters rebellions would occur and these were a sign that heaven was displeased and was withdrawing its mandate. So the Emperor did his best to maintain stability.

Another native Chinese religion which also started as a philosophy but gradually turned into a system of worship was Taoism. This grew up at the same time as Confucianism but it held the opposite view. The Taoists worshipped nature and felt that everything happened in the right way if man did not interfere; the reasons changed, things were born and died in a natural cycle. They felt that "inaction" was the best policy.

A third religion, Buddhism, entered China from India about 1000 years ago. Buddhism, like Taoism, preached a withdrawal from the world, and it seems to have appealed to many people because its ceremonies were more extravagant and more satisfying than those of the existing religions. Buddhist temples became immensely rich, as many people left all their possessions to them and because temples were not taxed. In the eighth century, the Emperor persecuted Buddhists savagely because he was suspicious of the wealth and power of these temples. Though Buddhism waned in importance as an independent religion from then on, it became part of popular belief.

Two other religions entered China later: Islam and Christianity. Islam is still the dominant religion in the northwest of China but after unrest in the area in the eighteenth century many Chinese Muslims moved east. Even today, every village in China has at least one Muslim restaurant, where pork is not served, and butchers have separate counters for this and other meats to avoid upsetting Muslims. Christian missionaries arrived much later, in the seventeenth century, 1000 years after Islam, and had most effect in the areas once occupied by Western powers along the eastern coast.

Today's Government in China is officially atheist and is trying to break free from the traditions of the past.

RECENT HISTORY

In 1949 and throughout the 1950s, China struggled to re-establish industry, a priority for a Communist Party, the party of the industrial worker. Until 1960, the Soviet Union had provided most of China's technical advice. But in 1960 Mao's determination to socialize agriculture against Russian wishes (they felt he should first deal with industry along the lines set down by Marx and Lenin) led to a break with the Soviet Union. This developed into a power struggle between the two great Communist powers over who should lead the Communist bloc. China was forced to become self-reliant, but the rejection of the outside world had serious repercussions for Western-educated specialists, particularly during the Cultural Revolution (1966-76), when Mao Zedong led a campaign to clean up the Communist Party, which he thought had become corrupt and over-privileged. Since the late nineteenth century, young Chinese had been going abroad to learn about the new technological achievements of the West, whether in architecture, industrial technology, scientific research or education and information science. During the Cultural Revolution, professionals who had been educated abroad were attacked as both over-privileged and subject to undesirable foreign influence. Specialists, in whatever field, were accused of seeking fame at the expense of the peasant masses and were forced to do agricultural labour or menial cleaning jobs to "reform their ideas".

When Mao died in 1976, the Cultural Revolution ended, and many Chinese hoped for dramatic changes in their lives. For some, these changes came quickly when the new leader, Deng Xiaoping, abolished the collectives and brigades in the countryside, and allowed peasant families to work the land allocated to them as family units. The ability of the family to make money for itself, over and above taxable production, unleashed a tremendous surge in agricultural output.

For professionals, too, the end of the Cultural Revolution meant a new freedom to practise their expertise, to research, to write, to perform without fear of criticism of "privilege". For those involved in transport, the increase in agricultural production meant more work, more bonuses, more opportunities (though it also meant more headaches for the planners, who had to improve overstretched facilities).

For workers in industry, the end of the Cultural Revolution meant the end of political incentives, and the beginning of financial incentives which, if they worked harder, meant an improvement in their living standards. The new stress on productivity rather than political purity also meant that factory management had to improve and make production more efficient in order to achieve the greater productivity that would benefit both the State and the factory workers.

OVERPOPULATION AND UNEMPLOYMENT

During the later years of the Cultural Revolution Mao realized the urgent need to curb China's fast-growing population if the country was to avoid famine. Couples were encouraged (and in some places, forced) to have a gap of four years between the two children that were considered the ideal number. Then, in the late 1970s, the single-child policy was introduced. The policy will not be enforced indefinitely – the problem is most acute now as the unchecked families of the early and mid-1960s are reaching marrying age. Nevertheless, there has been an alarming rise in female infanticide in recent years as traditional families want to have sons to carry on the line. In some rural areas the normal ratio of boys to girls in the under-five age-group has been completely reversed, as girl babies are drowned at birth so that the unfortunate mother can try again to have the son so vital to the peasant farmer.

Though unemployment is not a problem in rural areas, in the towns there were and still are, not enough jobs for the thousands of young people who finish their education every year. During the Cultural Revolution, school and university graduates were sent off to the countryside, where more hands were always welcome and where, it was hoped, young city-dwellers would learn revolutionary enthusiasm and hard work from the peasants. They stayed in the countryside for a minimum of two years and on their return were gradually absorbed into the workforce. But some were forced to stay in the distant rural areas against their will. When Mao died many returned from their "exile", confident that the reversal of the Cultural Revolution policies meant that they could return to city life. They, and successive groups of school-leavers, have not all been allocated jobs, as there are simply not enough

Poster advocating the one-child family policy.

to go round. In some cases, parents arrange to take early retirement on condition that their child will be given a job in the same factory. Others have been encouraged to set up small "service" industries, selling hot snacks, repairing bicycles or cutting hair by the roadside.

MODERN ATTITUDES TOWARDS WORK

The generation of those educated during the Cultural Revolution continues to present difficulties, for its members feel let down by the Government, and they are cynical about politics and unmoved by moral pressure. Their education was disrupted by the policy of "putting politics in command", which meant that they spent little time on academic work and now see those educated after 1976 passing them by and going into interesting and skilled jobs for which they have not been trained. During the Cultural Revolution they were deafened by political messages and they now take no notice of authority.

Their enthusiasm for material goods has brought about great changes in China. Where once, especially during the Cultural Revolution, possessions were not to be sought, where personal adornment could lead to punishment, now young men walk through the streets carrying huge tape-recorders and wearing imported sun-glasses with the maker's label still stuck on (to prove that they really came from the fashionable West), and girls wear short skirts with high-heeled shoes, curl their hair and wear make-up.

This generation was the first to reject the army as an honoured career, preferring to try and find a job in which money, rather than glory, could be made. And today's university graduates are also much more interested in money than their more idealistic parents. This attitude to work, where making money is seen as perhaps more important than the patriotic goal of building the country and contributing to the general raising of living standards, will certainly affect the prestige of certain types of job. It is ironic that money should be valued so highly in China, where 2000 years ago the merchant class was despised as lower than peasants and artisans.

A communal kitchen. This kitchen is shared by three families in a block of flats in Shanghai. Each has their own stove and storage space, but it is strange in a country that sets much store by good food that the kitchens are so neglected.

AGRICULTURE

The Temple of Heaven in Peking, built for the emperors to conduct ceremonies praying for good harvests and to house the ancestral tablets of the imperial family.

For thousands of years the majority of the Chinese people have worked in the fields as peasants, sowing and harvesting according to the varying climate of the vast country in which they live. The importance of agriculture to the rulers of ancient China lay in the taxation system. Grain and regional products were collected as tax by local officials and sent to the capital. As long as there were no natural disasters, and as long as the local officials and the imperial house did not demand too much from the peasants, the country remained at peace. If tax demands were too heavy peasants often had to leave their land, for they could not afford to buy seed or keep themselves. They would often band together in armies, to rob others and occasionally attack the cities. Such bands of landless peasants could be used by those who wanted to overthrow the government, so it was in the interests of the Emperor to maintain agricultural prosperity.

The Emperor's interest in agriculture was symbolically demonstrated by his ceremonial initiation of the agricultural year, when, each spring, he ploughed eight furrows in the grounds of the Temple of Agriculture in Peking. Chinese calendars today still carry the ancient agricultural terms for the months, which include phrases like "corn rain", "grain full", "grain in the ear" as well as descriptions of the characteristic weather: "frost's descent", "great heat", "beginning of autumn", "stopping of heat".

Today, about 70% of China's population of 1000 million still lives by agriculture and the contribution of the peasants to the national economy is still vital. Life for China's peasants varies tremendously as the country is so vast. Stretching from the frozen North-East, which borders Siberia, to the sub-tropical South, where rubber,

Terraced fields in Sichuan. In many parts of China farmers are becoming lazy, as a result of the new agricultural policies, and are no longer bothering to terrace their fields. In the long term, the resulting erosion will be disastrous, further reducing the small amount of cultivable land available to feed a billion people. Trees have their lower branches lopped off for firewood, giving a tufty look to the top.

coffee and pineapples grow, China's climatic variation is considerable. From West to East, from the Himalayas to the sea, the Yangtze ("long") river passes through the narrow gorges of the mountains east of the fertile Sichuan basin, winding through the poor province of Anhui and the rich rice and silk areas of Jiangsu to the commercial centre of Shanghai.

In the North, around and to the north of Peking, and in the North-West, the ground is frozen for two or three months in winter and the peasants have to work in greenhouses or look after their livestock whilst they cannot till the fields. Though the winter is hard, the freezing weather kills many pests and the less strenuous work is something of a rest for many peasants. In the South, by contrast, the cycle of planting and harvesting never ceases: three grain crops and an endless succession of vegetable and fruit harvests allow the peasants to become relatively rich but provide back-breaking labour throughout the 12 months of the year.

For peasants in China, and for city workers, China's system of government provides the framework within which they work. In 1949, the Chinese Communist Party, led by Mao Zedong, overthrew the Nationalist Government of Chiang Kai-shek, to establish the People's Republic of China.

The country was in a state of almost total collapse. Agriculture had been severely disrupted by 40 years of civil war, when many peasants had fled from their land before the advancing armies. In many areas the Japanese and the Chinese Nationalists, both determined to stop the Communist advance, had practised the same "three alls" policy: kill all the people, destroy all the crops and loot all the valuables. Those who managed to survive these massacres found themselves without their means of livelihood. The reform of agriculture was the first task of the new Government, for it was essential to get the peasants to return to their fields to provide the food necessary for the population.

Land belonging to landlords and "rich" peasants (those who could afford to employ others to work for them) was seized by the Government and distributed equally amongst the poorer peasants. As the poorer peasants possessed very few tools and draught animals, they were formed into mutual aid teams and resources were pooled. Working collectively, and using the scarce

In south and south-west China the water buffalo is the major draught animal. On the wet fields used for rice mechanization is difficult, but water-buffaloes like mud. Here a field, first ploughed by the buffalo, is harrowed and smoothed, ready for a winter crop. The old man is wearing a long apron, the characteristic men's costume in the south-western province of Sichuan.

resources in their locality, the peasants gradually re-established agricultural production. Between 1954 and 1955 the mutual aid teams were formed into larger groupings called "agricultural producers' co-operatives", comprising about 30 to 40 families and often coinciding with existing villages. As these co-operatives were larger than the mutual aid teams, they could carry out bigger schemes for land improvement during the slack season, building small dams and canals, improving irrigation schemes and transport facilities, as well as being able to afford more machinery and draught animals. These co-operatives were gradually formed into a third grouping, the "higher producers' co-operatives", which appeared between 1956 and 1957. These were yet larger, consisting of between 100 and 300 families, and were different in that all land was collectively owned and all income now depended solely on the amount of work done.

The next, and longer-lived, stage of agricultural organization was the formation of the "people's communes": once again, larger groupings than those that had gone before. An average commune might comprise about 25,000 people and was the basic form of government in the region, responsible for collecting taxes, controlling local resources, running schools, banks, kindergartens, clinics and small hospitals, and other necessary local services. The peasants continued to work the land they were allocated and to be paid for that work. They had small vegetable plots on which they could grow vegetables for themselves, and could keep a small number of animals, but otherwise their produce went to the commune and eventually to the central government. This was the tax the peasants paid.

The system of communes still persists, but since 1976 there has been a change in the way that peasants work within the communes. The new system was first tried experimentally

Against the familiar limestone landscape of Guilin, young men spread out nets in a fish farm. Though fish has always been a vital and highly prized part of the Chinese diet, fish-farming on a grand scale is comparatively recent. Sea-fishing is also common but the fresh-water carp is the most popular fish in China today and fish-farming is very profitable.

Gathering in fish at a fish farm. Every small pond, especially in the south, is now given over to the sale of fish. The fish are usually taken to market alive as this is a guarantee of the freshness necessary in Chinese cooking.

the proceeds of her egg sales.

There are problems, however, which mean that the Government may have to intervene and exercise more control, particularly over what crops are grown. Many peasants have stopped growing rice and wheat because they can make more money selling vegetables in the towns. If not enough grain is produced China will have to buy expensive grains from abroad instead of making money by exporting rice. The Government are also having problems implementing their one-child policy under the family responsibility system, because the larger the family the greater the potential wealth.

But, although more Government intervention in agriculture is expected it is unlikely that the new system of working in family units will be abandoned, as it is very popular and produces better results than those achieved during the last years of commune production. It was important to organize the peasants in increasingly large communal units during the early years of the People's Republic, for they made possible the large-scale construction of schools, hospitals, roads, canals and all the buildings necessary for the running of rural life. Now that these have been started the peasants can contribute to their maintenance by paying their taxes, instead of directly helping to build and run them.

in a few areas but has gradually spread all over the country. Now, peasant families can make many of the decisions about what they grow on the land they are allocated. They must give a percentage of their produce to the State (through the commune) as taxation, but after that they are free to grow, and more importantly to sell, what they can.

In the first years the experiment proved a great success: agricultural production soared dramatically and some peasants grew very rich if they were lucky in their land (and also if they were lucky in being near a city where they could sell their produce easily), to the point where one peasant in 1984 bought a Toyota saloon car on

THE RICH PEASANT FAMILY

The Liu family has never known a better year. Their farmhouse on the outskirts of the capital city of Sichuan province, Chengdu, is a smart, two-storey building decorated with yellow and green tiles and provided with running water (cold) and clean tiled floors instead of the damp earth floors they used to have in the old house.

There are 11 members of the Liu family living in the new house, all but the very youngest helping to contribute to the wealth of the family, which is considerable. Lin Han says that they are almost a 10,000 *yuan* household, a term used to refer to "peasant millionaires". Their income is derived from two sources: agriculture and industry. Old Mr and Mrs Liu were originally peasants, but Liu Han, one of their two sons, was quick to seize on the new opportunities offered for individual enterprise in 1976. He realized that the

New houses near Guangzhou (Canton). Typical older houses can be seen behind, with a line of painted decoration along the gable. As peasants get richer they are building new houses called "foreign houses" like the three-storied, tiled mansion with balconies.

Chinese had for the past ten years been starved of bright and cheerful clothing because of the puritannical ideas of the Cultural Revolution and now that policies had changed there was a potential market for it in the nearby city. He made a few enquiries in Chengdu and finally bought a roll of bright cotton from a factory that made sportswear. He got his wife, a clever seamstress, to cut out a polo-necked sweater (copied from one he'd seen a tourist from Hong Kong wearing) and make it up. Old Mrs Liu oversewed all the seams to stop them fraying and the basis of the Liu family's wealth was established. Soon Liu Han had enough money to buy some special sewing machines for the women in the family. He started a market stall in Chengdu and one of his nieces took it over when he became too busy contacting factories for supplies and cousins in distant cities for new trade outlets.

While this furious sewing goes on by night, the family's fields have to be tended by day. The Lius are lucky. It is said that if you were to plant a broom handle in the rich soil of the Chengdu plain it would grow. All the year round there are vegetables of all sorts. One crop succeeds another and the year is a continual round of sewing seed, weeding, harvesting, ploughing and sewing again. All the work, except for the ploughing, is done by the women of the family, often with a toddler strapped to their backs as they bend over their green seedlings. In the evening they rush home, ready to spend a few hours sewing T-shirts and polo-necks for Liu Han.

He is planning to build a factory. He has made enough money to pay for its construction and is confident that, with several cousins exploring new market outlets in other cities in Sichuan province (which has a population of 100 million) and beyond, he can afford to expand. The business has finally outgrown the family, although it will remain a source of family wealth. Liu Han is thinking of employing a few local women to work full-time in his new factory. The new draft employment law was drawn up in order to allow small enterprises like this to expand, without working against the population control policy. If he could not employ people Liu Han would have gone on making use of relatives and would certainly have broken the family planning law by having a lot of children to help with the work. Since the only punishment is a fine Liu Han could afford to ignore it as he is making a lot of money. To some Chinese it seems strange that in a socialist country one individual can

Mealtime. Food is one of the great sources of conversation and interest in China. Every region has its speciality, though fish, here placed centrally, is highly prized everywhere.

employ (and possibly therefore exploit) another, but Liu Han is not bothered by the politics of the new policies: he is just determined to make the most of them.

Liu Han's younger brother divides his time between the fields and the fabrics. He does the ploughing and heavy agricultural work, and also does a lot of the delivery work for the garment enterprise. His wife tends the fields by day and works at her sewing machine at night, just like Liu Han's wife, whose eldest girl has already begun to help sewing the straight seams, although she is only 12.

Because of their relative wealth, the Liu family spend a great deal on their occasional family feasts. At Chinese New Year, old Mrs Liu starts cooking two or three days in advance (partly because it is considered unlucky to cook on New Year's Day but partly because there is so much food to be prepared), and every corner of the kitchen and sitting room is piled with fragrant dishes of pork and soya, chicken in rice wine, peppery bean curd and eggs cooked in tea, neatly covered and waiting for the great day. Plenty of wine is available for the relatives who crowd into the house to share in the wealth that they help to create.

THE POOR PEASANT FAMILY

The Ma family live in Shanxi province, in a village set high on a hillside in the dusty yellow foothills of the Wutai mountains. The mountains are not particularly high but they are bare and barren, and cold winds blow over

A peasant house near Wutaishan, Shanxi province. In the bare, deforested landscape of Shanxi life is quite hard. The winters are cold and little agricultural work can be done. Inside the house there is a hollow brick platform which is heated by the cooking stove flue which passes underneath it. In winter the family sit on it and they sleep on it all year round.

them in the dry winters and the ground freezes hard. Three generations of Mas live together in a farmhouse built of yellow earth with pressed earth walls topped by grey tiles. Within the yard there are pigsties and mounds of fodder for the animals in winter. Apart from the pigs the Ma family tend a mixed herd of sheep and cattle, cattle whose thick reddish fur grows long in the freezing winters.

The oldest member of the family is Grandfather Ma. After years working out on the hills, he is now almost crippled by arthritis and spends much of the winter lying on the brick bed, kept warm by a small stove underneath. In summer he sits outside in the warm sun. His wife boils up soups of medicinal herbs prescribed by the local doctor, a specialist in traditional Chinese medicine. The medicinal broth is intended to lessen the pain of arthritis a little and is cheaper than Western drugs. Old Mrs Ma looks after the house, cleans and sweeps up every day and feeds the pigs. She prepares the meals when the rest of the family are out.

Their son, Ma Dahan, has taken over his father's work as a herdsman. Every day he drives his flock on to the hillside and then keeps watch over them all day. Most of the flock, both sheep and cattle, go to the State as his tax payment and the remainder he now sells in the nearby markets. He always makes sure he has some fat sheep ready for when the Mongolian Buddhists come to the temples in Wu Tai in early spring. Though they come to worship (Wu Tai mountain is supposed to be the home of their most revered *boddhisattva*), and though Buddhists are meant to be vegetarians, the Mongolians are very fond of mutton and are prepared to spend a little extra on food when on holiday.

Ma Dahan's wife looks after their small vegetable patch, where she grows food for the family and a few special medicinal herbs. These, though difficult to grow, can fetch quite a lot of money in the local markets. As more and more Chinese begin to travel, and as the Wu Tai mountain now receives quite a few tourists, especially those from Hong Kong who still prefer to use traditional remedies, Mrs Ma can make a few *yuan* selling her medicinal herbs outside the major temples. The problem is that she has a long journey to the temple. She has to walk quite a way to the road, carrying a heavy basket, and then wait for the bus. The bus doesn't cost more than a few pence but it is both full and slow. Mrs Ma often has to put her precious basket of herbs on the roof of the bus because she cannot squeeze it inside. The seats in the bus are worn out and it is uncomfortable sitting on the threadbare upholstery for two or three hours. Even when she arrives in the main street, below the great temple, she has to walk round to the entrance and sit there, hoping that no one will ask for the trading permit she hasn't got and hoping, too, that plenty of Hong Kong tourists will arrive that day.

The Mas have two children: a boy of

A donkey cart in the North. The bare, flat landscape of the North China Plain shows how difficult life can be there for the peasants. Once the winter wheat is sown, there is little to be done until the spring, as the ground freezes over. In rural areas, animals are important in transportation.

eleven and a girl of seven. They both go to school most days, although when Ma Dahan goes to market with the animals, his son has to stay behind to take the remainder out to pasture.

Life is hard for the Ma family. They don't benefit much from the new freedom for peasants to grow what they like and get rich. They live in a cold and barren mountainous area where few vegetables grow and where transport is difficult. All the hay they cut for the animals for winter feed has to be carried to the farm on their own backs; all the vegetables grown in their little plot have to be carried down the hill to the house; and all the animal manure Mrs Ma uses on her plot has to be carried up the hill.

In the winter, the animals need daily attention but Mrs Ma's vegetable plot is frozen. She and her mother-in-law sew cloth shoes for the family and make their summer cotton jackets and trousers. Mrs Ma prepares her bundles of dried herbs and mushrooms for sale in the market.

They eat millet, gruel and maize buns with a few root vegetables stewed together in a couple of drops of precious (and expensive) soya sauce and oil. Very occasionally, when Mr Ma has been to market and sold some sheep, they have a little meat with their meal; this marks a special day in the otherwise monotonous year of back-breaking work.

INDUSTRY

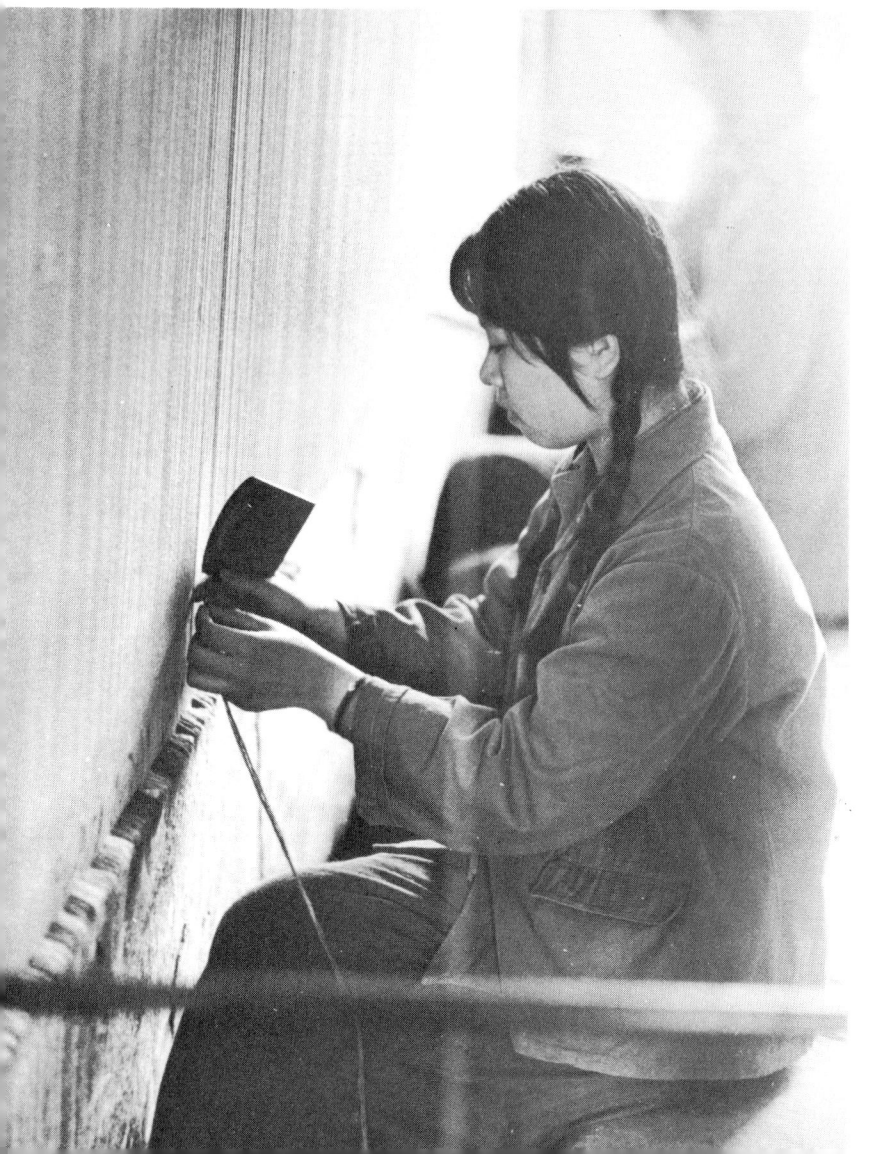

A carpet factory. Chinese carpets are still hand-made as labour is cheap in China. The thick pile of the carpet is later cut with scissors around the patterns to give a sculpted effect, and most of the carpets are exported.

State control of industry has a long history in China. As early as the Han dynasty (206 B.C. — A.D. 220), the Imperial Government controlled the salt and iron mines and able-bodied men were required not only to serve in the army but to do periods of manual labour in the mines and on construction sites such as the Great Wall. Until the nineteenth century, however, China's industry remained largely unmechanized, and such industrial enterprises as were founded in the nineteenth century were mainly concentrated on the eastern seaboard, around cities like Shanghai which had grown up with the arrival of Western traders.

Just before the Communists took over in 1949, the heavy industrial plants of the North-East had been stripped by the Russians in an attempt to take control of the area. Most of the rich Chinese who had owned factories in Shanghai and other coastal cities fled as the Communists advanced, leaving a managerial and entrepreneurial vacuum.

Thus, in 1949, the new Government faced the task of reorganizing China's cities along socialist lines. It was essential to try and incorporate such industrial enterprises and managers as remained into the new system and to clean up such problems as the tens of thousands of prostitutes in Shanghai (who were eventually "re-educated" to become factory workers and respectable citizens). Initially the Government attempted to get factories back to work under the control of management committees consisting of members of the army, worker delegates and exisiting managers. Then, in 1956, a national wage scale was introduced and those factory owners who had remained in China finally became share-owning managers, participating in the management and profit of their factories rather than taking all the profits, as they had done before.

From this period, China became virtually self sufficient industrially. All essential light industrial products were home-produced and virtually all other industrial requirements could be satisfied by Chinese production. The problem was often one of quality: consumers preferred better-designed imported items, and the more sophisticated technology of, for example, the jet engine, was beyond the resources of China's experts and machines.

With the coming of the Cultural Revolution, however, industry underwent a further reorganization. Many of the former factory owners who had continued to work as managers in their factories because of their skills, were denounced as capitalists and made to clean floors and do other dirty jobs. Workers' positions did not change dramatically but they were expected to work, not for material things like more money, but for the good of the country and the Communist Party.

By the early 1970s this atmosphere of purity with its high moral tone was clearly beginning to pall. Workers wanted improvements in their standard of living; they wanted better wages and the chance to make even more money. Although material incentives were re-introduced in 1976 after the death of Mao, workers are clearly still not happy about the restrictions of rules, the low wage scales and the impossibility of bettering themselves. They see some peasants getting rich very quickly (a great deal of publicity was given to the egg-selling peasant lady who bought her Japanese car in 1984), which is impossible for them, even with small bonuses for better work.

The government is still uncertain as to what to do about the pay of workers (both blue-collar and white-collar). When changes do come they are likely to include the possibility of the sack (for not working hard enough) to counter-balance any pay rise offered. While the peasants in the countryside, working once again as family units, feel the state has less influence on their daily lives, for those who live and work in the cities, the constraints of rules and regulations are felt more strongly than ever.

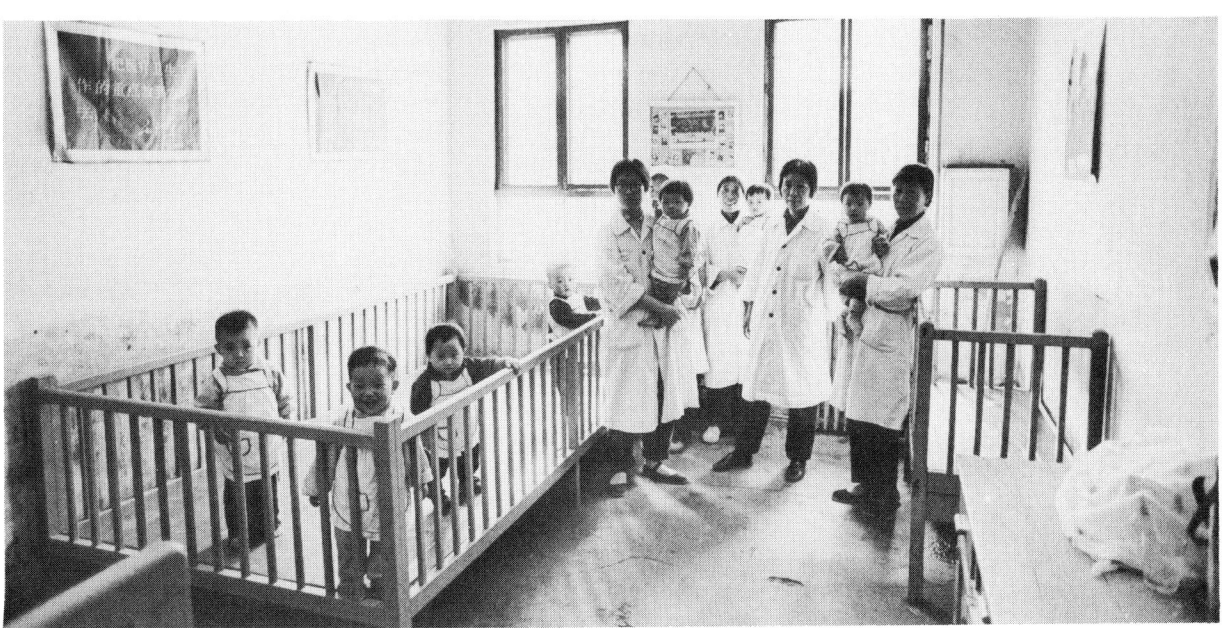

A factory crèche. As most young women work, child-care is very important and all large institutions have their own crèches, kindergartens, and sometimes even schools. But some young people still prefer to leave their child with a relative for individual attention and care.

THE SILK-REELING FACTORY WORKER

Chen Xiaoming is 26 and works in the silk-reeling factory in Suzhou. She began work there when she left school at 17 and has worked at various tasks before settling to the reeling work she does now. She works eight hours a day, six days a week. Xiaoming's day off is Wednesday, the same day as her husband. Factories in China usually work three eight-hour shifts a day, seven days a week, so workers have different days off, spread throughout the week. A great headache for factory administrators is to try and organize days off for their workers which coincide with those of their spouses. Though holidays for workers are not yet widespread it is likely that in the near future workers will get an annual holiday of a week or two. Now they get a few days off at the Chinese New Year and a day off for International Labour Day on 1 May and National Day on 1 October.

Suzhou is a pretty city in the heart of the silk-producing area of China, on the Yangtse delta. The countryside outside the city is criss-crossed with canals and bright green with rice seedlings in glistening paddy fields. Inside the white-washed farmhouses one room is usually set aside for silkworms. They are kept on great round straw trays and fed on mulberry leaves picked from the low bushes grown specially for the purpose. In a few weeks the grubs grow into big fat caterpillars, eating leaves at a great rate, and as they prepare to spin their silken cocoons they are moved to a bamboo lattice. The caterpillars climb up the lattice and begin to spin the silk thread round and round themselves, until it is a hard white case about the size of a bantam's egg.

The cocoons are sold to the silk-reeling factories in nearby cities. There they are sorted and quality checked before being dropped into troughs of hot water in front of the reeling machines. Chen Xiaoming and her workmates who sit alongside her at the noisily rattling machines have to feel in the hot water for the ends of the silk as the cocoons begin to unravel. When they have found a silken thread they attach it to a revolving bobbin which reels in the silk. Then they search for another, keeping their eyes on all the bobbins to make sure they are reeling smoothly.

The cocoons bob in the hot water as Chen Xiaoming feels deftly for a fine thread. Her fingers are white and water-swollen at the end of the day, as if she had been in the bath too long, but she has got used to it. Some girls cannot stand it and have to give up if they get allergic reactions or badly chapped hands. They have tried using gloves, but the silk threads are so fine they cannot be felt through gloves. They have tried cooling the water, but then the silk doesn't reel off easily and tends to snap. So far there seems to be no substitute for bare hands in hot water. When the first reeling is done the silk bobbins are reeled several times more to prepare them for machine spinning. Some are dyed; others bleached; some are left the pale butter colour of natural silk. The reels then go to a mill where silk fabrics are woven.

Chen Xiaoming married last year and would like to have a baby, but she has been told by the family planning office of the factory that she must wait. Her husband, who is two years older than her, is a supervisor in a machine-tool factory; he, too, feels that they should wait. Chen is almost tempted to ignore the rules but the management in her factory has threatened to stop all the bonuses for all the workers if one single person breaks the family planning rules. Xiaoming doesn't know if they would actually do it but she is not prepared to risk it.

Xiaoming and her husband live in a small flat near the machine-tool factory, part of the housing the factory provides for its workers. Xiaoming has a 20-minute bicycle ride to get to work, but they took the flat near her

Crowded housing in Xiamen. When young people get married they hope to get a flat with at least one room. Owing to lack of space, the balcony becomes another "room" as well as a laundry. Single and divorced people often have to live in dormitories at their place of work.

husband's factory as they would otherwise have had to stay in single-sex dormitories for unmarried workers. The rent for the two-roomed flat, with its sunny balcony where Xiaoming does the cooking, costs them about 3% of their joint income of 110 *yuan* a month. The rent includes water and electricity, though there is talk of installing meters now that people have more and more electric gadgets like televisions, tape-recorders and (still in rare cases) fridges and washing machines. As Suzhou is south of the Yangtse there is no central heating in the block, for the weather is not thought to be cold enough. The temperature can often hover around freezing during the winter, however, but as no one has any central heating Xiaoming and her husband cannot really complain.

A standpipe in Shanghai. New houses in cities have running water but many people still have to rely on public pipes like this for water for washing, cleaning and cooking.

Chen Xiaoming is not ambitious: all she wants is a nice flat and a comfortable life, but her husband would like to get on. He is not yet quite certain in which direction he wants his career to develop but he knows that it will depend on a lot of factors, some of them out of his control. Every evening he reads books on business management because this is a new field in China. The manager of Xiaoming's factory used to be the owner of it but the Government took it over in 1956. He stayed on as manager because he knew how to run the business and because, unlike the factory owners who left their businesses in 1949, he wanted to try and help the industrial development of China under Mao Zedong. During the Cultural Revolution, he was dismissed as manager and made to clean the floors and attend endless meetings where he was made to wear a dunce's hat and listen to accusations that he had cheated the workers and stolen money. In 1976 he was reinstated and, though he is over retiring age, still acts as manager because his expertise is invaluable.

Xiaoming's husband knows that people like this are now few and far between and that there are not enough middle-aged factory managers with the right experience or go-ahead outlook. China is trying to streamline her industry and increase exports, but few people have either the ideas or the daring to stick their necks out and do it. One of Xiaoming's husband's heroes is the famous manager of a shirt factory in Anhui who practised Western business management methods, sacking bad workers, promoting good ones, finding out what his clients wanted and becoming a national success story. Xiaoming's husband would like to follow the example of the shirt-maker and make a lot of money through exports. Sometimes he goes to Shanghai to international trade exhibitions to see what sort of products other countries produce and he tries to think up ways of competing with them. It isn't easy because there are so many Government hurdles to get over and so much paperwork to face. While Chen Xiaoming's husband plans expansion and improvements in the machine-tool industry Xiaoming dreams of a fridge and washing machine.

THE EMBROIDERY FACTORY WORKER

Mrs Ma works in an embroidery factory in the south-western town of Chengdu in Sichuan province. The province, though not a major silk-growing area, is connected to the silk-producing provinces by the Yangtse River and has for many centuries been renowned for its brocade weaving. Silk embroidery is almost as old as brocade weaving but has received a boost in recent years from the tourist industry.

Mrs Ma has been working as an embroiderer for five years. She was selected when she left school at 16 because she was nimble-fingered and neat in her work. At first, she simply worked on other people's embroideries, filling in areas of blocked colour with running stitch. Later, she began to complete whole embroideries herself, varying the stitches and colours a little as she thought appropriate. Recently, she has begun to participate in design meetings, advising on the sorts of effects that can be produced, modifying over-elaborate designs and making her own suggestions.

The majority of the embroideries produced at the factory are for export. Many are bought by tourists who come to visit the factory and watch the fine work being done in the light, sunny rooms; more are sent to big stores abroad, where they are framed

A finisher at work in an embroidery workshop, Xi'an.

and sold, and some of the finest examples are taken by provincial and national leaders to present to their hosts when they go to foreign countries on trade delegations.

The designs for embroidery are produced in the factory itself, by graduates from the Sichuan Provincial Art School. Most of the designs are based on traditional painting themes: bird in reeds, goldfish swimming amongst slender waterweeds and pandas in bamboo groves. Pandas are native to Sichuan province and many of the tourists who visit the factory will buy small embroidered pictures of pandas as a souvenir. Occasionally, the factory will produce larger pictures to order, mostly for presentations abroad or for office buildings and reception rooms.

Mrs Ma's wages are fixed by the

Grandfather and grand-daughter. In southern China it is common to eat out of doors, sitting on low bamboo chairs. The care and supervision of children is often the daily responsibility of retired grandparents, who also help with household chores while their children are at work.

Provincial Handicrafts Bureau which runs the factory. She gets a small bonus for producing extra work above her set quota. The quota is not set very high as the work is fine, hard on the eyes and back, and requires a great deal of concentration. The workers have many short breaks to stretch their aching backs and relieve their eyes and, often, because tourist groups are coming round with their flash cameras. The tourists want to come and peer closely at the fine work of the embroiderers — especially the two-sided embroideries, where each side of the work is different but no loose ends betray the separate pictures — and it is easy for them to jog an embroiderer and spoil a stitch, so the workers don't do any fine work when tourists are in the building.

Mrs Ma had a son last year. He is now ten months old and stays at home with her mother-in-law when she comes to work. Occasionally, when the old lady has to go to the doctor, Mrs Ma brings him to work, where all the other embroiderers play with him and the tourists give him sweets. Mrs Ma was given six months' leave on full pay after the birth of her son but is now back at work, with no loss of seniority. Six months' maternity leave on full pay is a recent innovation, to enable mothers to spend more time with their precious single baby under the "one-child family" regulations.

THE COALMINER

Han Wenming is a coalminer of 56. He is about to take early retirement so that his younger son, who has been out of work for four years, can be given a job in the coal mine in his place. Han Wenming has worked in the mine near Datong in north-western China for 40 years and will get a pension when he retires. Retiring age is 60 for men and 55 for women, but since the unemployment problem of recent years people are beginning to arrange early retirement in the way that Mr Han has, so that their children can get jobs in their place. There are not enough jobs for the millions of school-leavers every year and there is no Government scheme to offer these young people any money whilst they "wait for work", a term that Chinese officials use instead of "unemployed". They have to rely on their families for

This little low house in Datong, with its decorative windows, is typical of North China. The windows are made of paper and there is no water supply or toilet; the inhabitants have to go out to the public lavatories and a standpipe in the street.

Loading coal on the outskirts of Datong. A temporary form of transport, a cart hitched to a bicycle, is used to carry coal for personal consumption. Coal is the major industrial and domestic fuel in the north of China and causes considerable pollution, particularly at mealtimes, when every chimney in every little house belches out smoke.

pocket-money, clothing and food, and most Chinese families do not have much money to spare.

Mr Han is an experienced coal-face worker in one of China's most modern mines, which is quite heavily mechanized. His son will only earn about 30 *yuan* a month when he starts work, just under a third of his father's wages. Once he has learnt the job, however, his wages will rise and he will be able to earn a little extra for greater productivity.

Every day, Mr Han reports for work at 7.30 a.m. and takes his protective clothing out of his locker. It is very cold underground so he puts on two layers of thick cotton underwear under his heavy black overalls. Much of the mine is damp underfoot so he wears wellington boots. He wears a standard safety helmet with a lamp attached to a battery worn on his belt. Together with the others on his shift he walks, with some difficulty in his heavy clothing, to the pithead, where they take the lift down. Below ground they have to walk quite a distance to the area they are working: a vast underground cave where coal dust hangs in the air and the muffled sound of underground blasting echoes.

At 11.30 Mr Han goes back up in the lift to the locker-room, where he leaves his helmet and outer clothes and boots before having lunch in the canteen. Like most other workers he goes back to work after a short nap at home after lunch. The lunch-time siesta is an old habit in China and though the Government is trying to discourage it, as they feel it wastes time with workers cycling back home for a nap, offices closing down and taxi-drivers snoozing in their cars, the old habit dies hard and many people find it really hard to keep awake after lunch.

In the evening, when he has finished his shift, he showers in the communal bath-house before going home for supper. His wife has never had a job but she is always busy. They live in a flat in one of the blocks of apartments

built by the mine for workers and their families. Retired miners can stay on in their flats, so there are quite a number of old people to be cared for and this is part of Mrs Han's "voluntary" work.

A neighbourhood committee has been set up by the mine to look after the welfare of the miners and their families who live adjacent to the pit. The committee members, who are unpaid, are mostly housewives and recently retired people. Regular matters of concern are hygiene and street-sweeping, and another task, on which they work with the local policeman, is security. The committee wants to prevent theft by encouraging people to look after their possessions and to be on the look-out for suspicious people or incidents. The committee also makes sure there are rotas of people, like Mrs Han, to shop and clean for those who are elderly or sick. It is the custom in China for family members to go to hospital to help feed and wash a sick relative but if there is no one to do this, the committee will send Mrs Han to do the job. The committee runs a couple of small clinics for first-aid, which also do much to inform people about health and hygiene and, especially, family planning.

The coal mine has its own family planning scheme, based on the number of employees and dependants of marriageable age, and it has a target for the number of babies born every year. All newly wed couples get a visit from one of the health-workers from the clinic, who explains the various methods of contraception. Even then, the young couple will have to wait until it is their turn, according to the plan to have a baby. When they have had their one child at the appointed time, the health-visitor will call again to try and ensure that they don't have any more, so that the coal mine's target is not spoiled. Part of the neighbourhood committee's work consists in supporting this family planning scheme with follow-up visits, which can be very persistent.

Like the local policeman, Mrs Han knows everybody in the block and everyone in the neighbouring blocks, too. While people grumble behind her back if she comes to tell them to tidy up their firewood or not to leave their bicycles on the landing, they know that if they fall ill or cannot cope in some way she will bustle round to help.

When Mr Han gets back from work Mrs Han is usually there with supper ready for him. She occasionally has to go out after supper to see a sick neighbour or attend a meeting but most evenings she cooks and then washes up at the sink, with its one cold-water tap, before sitting down with her knitting to watch television with her husband and two sons.

Mr Han has also sometimes to attend meetings after work, as he is a member of the Communist Party at the coal mine. He feels it is an honour to have been asked to apply for membership, and an even greater honour to have been accepted. Both he and his wife are "active" in local affairs; they speak out and they get things done. They know they are not always popular with their neighbours but say that if you are going to take a leading role in society, as a good Party member should, you have to put up with a bit of criticism.

THE PROFESSIONS

In traditional China, law and government at the local level were both administered by one man, a local official appointed by the central imperial government. He had no training in administration: he obtained his rank by passing a series of examinations. Hundreds of applicants would be shut into specially built cells to write essays on Confucian topics. The essays were written in antiquated, stilted style and were based on years of learning the Confucian classics by heart. Though Confucius lived some 500 years B.C. his ideas on good government and correct conduct were still in force until 1911, when the last imperial dynasty was overthrown. A scholar had to master the classics and show a thorough knowledge of ancient poetry in order to pass the exams. The system was not unlike the old European tradition, when a knowledge of the Greek and Latin classics was considered more important than vocational training.

Though those days have passed, Chinese education still retains a great deal of rote learning, essential to master the complex written system. Most professionals in China today, however, have studied at universities which have been greatly influenced by the West, and their training is technical. Universities provide courses in the sciences and humanities, and other educational institutions provide vocational training. There are teacher training colleges in every province and specialized language-teaching institutes to train interpreters and tourist guides. Many of the teachers in these institutions were trained in the 1950s, a period of openness and scholarship.

Many of those who supported Mao and the Communist Party in the early days were idealistic young intellectuals and patriotic teachers who threw themselves into the reconstruction of their nation with enthusiasm. But, by the mid-1950s some began to feel constrained by Communist Party rules and others that reforms were not being properly carried out and that the Party needed direction and correction. There were many campaigns against intellectuals between 1955 and 1976. Some intellectuals suffered in each successive attack, being sent to the countryside for "re-education" through manual labour. Others were imprisoned and, during the most savage period, the ten years of the Cultural Revolution (1966-1976), some of China's foremost intellectuals, elderly professors of international stature, were persecuted to death. The Cultural Revolution was launched by Mao to clean up the Party, which he felt was becoming comfortable and corrupt, and to make education and culture more revolutionary. Thus many of the older generation of writers, poets, teachers and actors, often more liberal than Communist, suffered especially.

Today's professionals in China are amongst those who are most taken for granted. Their pay is determined by the State and is very low compared to that of factory workers, who now work to a bonus scheme to provide incentive for higher productivity. Though teachers were recently awarded a pay rise most professionals still barely earn enough to make ends meet. Prices are rising throughout China and they have no way of supplementing their income. They are usually highly motivated, and get a degree of job satisfaction denied to manual labourers, but they work long hours for small reward.

This lack of respect, in contrast with traditional China where intellectuals were considered superior, is probably the result of the Communist stress on industrial production. In all propaganda and literature, the productive worker, the creator of national wealth, is the hero. Teachers and doctors do not directly create wealth by making goods for sale and are not, therefore, held in high esteem.

THE LAWYER

Han Youfu is 31 and works as a lawyer in a suburban district of Peking. He has only been working as a lawyer for five years because it was not until the death of Mao and the downfall of the Gang of Four in 1976, that the work of lawyers was reinstated in China.

Han studied Chinese History at university and graduated in 1974. He was assigned to work in the administrative office of the Public Security Bureau of his Peking suburb. There, he worked on the registry of marriages. It was a routine secretarial job but it carried some responsibility, for, according to China's Marriage Law, Han had to make sure that the young couple who came to register their proposed marriage were there of their own accord. Before the twentieth century, it was the custom for Chinese parents to arrange their children's marriage. Though the young couple might never have seen each other before their wedding day these marriages were not necessarily unsuccessful, as it was in the interests of the parents to make the young couple happy. Great disgrace fell upon a family if there was a divorce and some young brides, desperately unhappy in their new homes, would throw themselves down wells or hang themselves, bringing shame upon their husband's family.

In the twentieth century young people began to read about freedom of choice and romantic love and fought against the traditional arranged marriage. When Mao took over the government of China in 1949 one of the first laws he passed was the Marriage Law, which insists that young people should marry out of choice, not because they have been forced into it by their parents.

Han Youfu took his duties in the Public Security Bureau very seriously and interrogated the young couples who came to see him. Not only did he want to know whether they had freely chosen each other, he also wanted to know how old they were, where they worked, whether they had permission to marry from their place of work, and the answers to other such questions.

In 1976, after the death of Mao, China began to set up the legal system that had only been operating in a small way since the beginning of the Cultural Revolution. Much had changed in those ten years. China was now interested in trade with the outside world and needed new trade regulations and tax laws. With the abolition of "people's courts", where people had in effect been tried by their neighbours, there was a new need for lawyers to represent people in court and to explain the law to them.

Han Youfu applied for permission to go back to university and study law so that he could be more useful in his job. He was also intrigued by the idea of building up a new legal system. His enthusiasm (and his record of hard

A legal check in a street market. People who feel that they have been cheated by being given underweight can report to this stall in the free market. Such legal aid to shoppers was unknown ten years ago, but now lawyers and the law have been revived in China, and citizens' rights are part of the new legalistic approach.

work) was such that he was recommended to go for further study. He knew he was lucky. In China it is a delicate problem: if you are very good at your job you are indispensable, so it is almost impossible to get another job or leave your place of work. Your employer can refuse to release you. Even if you have found another job you are powerless if your employer will not let you go. For Han, it was a question of persuading his superiors that he would definitely come back and that he would be of much more use to them after he had studied law at university for three years.

Han did go back to his old job after university, but now does a far wider range of things. His main function is to advise local residents about the law and their legal rights. Traditionally, the Chinese do not like to go to law: they prefer to deal with problems themselves. There is a sense that it is shameful to "show your dirty linen in public" by admitting that you need legal help. Because of this unwillingness Han holds open sessions throughout the summer, moving his desk outside into the street under an awning and setting up a great poster advertising "Legal Advice", hoping to attract the interest of passers-by.

After a day at his desk, advising people on all sorts of things – those accused of crimes who need lawyers to defend them; those who are victims of crime and need to take a case to court; those who are uncertain of their rights; and those who need support in the defence of their rights – Han Youfu bicycles home to his third-floor flat in a nearby residential block.

He carries his bike upstairs, locks it and leaves it on the landing outside the flat, because he feels that it is less likely to be stolen there. There has been a great increase in theft in China since 1976, as Mr Han knows from his work. During the Cultural Revolution it was almost a crime to want possessions and it was quite difficult to get away with theft. People were on their guard, watching each other, mainly for political reasons, and were well aware of what neighbours earned, what they owned and what they could afford. The sudden acquisition of another bicycle would not have passed unnoticed.

Since the end of the Cultural Revolution bonuses have been introduced in factories, young people have been encouraged to find what work they can, and people want material possessions. As it is now possible to earn a little more, and as many people saved a lot during the Cultural Revolution, there has been a great boom in consumer goods. The Hans have a colour television and a cassette recorder, both of which are covered with a cloth when not in use, to keep them away from prying eyes. Quite a few stories about burglaries have been circulating in their housing estate, so they lock the doors and windows carefully when they go out. Mr Han meets quite a few burglars through his work. Many of them are young, many of them unemployed and almost all of them are unmoved by politics, unaffected by the Party's moral teachings about honest hard work.

Mr Han is young enough to have

A young couple with their only daughter. The one-child family policy is essential if China is to maintain a balance between food production and population growth after the baby boom of the 1960s. Young city couples find it easier to accept, as there is so much pressure on space and time, and they dote on their children. There is concern that the present generation will grow up impossibly spoilt, as they are all only children.

had his education badly disrupted by the Cultural Revolution, so he has some sympathy with the young but he cannot understand their lack of interest in politics and their lack of drive. He feels that it is a generation gap and he worries about his daughter, who is only three now but whose education and upbringing as an only child are the major preoccupations of Mr Han and his wife. Mr Han was disappointed when she was born. Having accepted the Government's policy and agreed to have only one child he had hoped for a son, but as he saw more and more of the disaffected young men who had turned to crime he began to think that he was lucky. He says that girls are more gentle and better behaved and give their parents less cause for worry than boys.

On Sunday, which is his day off, Mr Han helps his wife with the family washing and then they go out, taking the little girl. Sometimes they take her tricycle to the local park; sometimes they take a bus out to the Summer Palace or to the Western Hills, wander around, buy their daughter an ice-cream or a bun, go boating on the lake or admire the displays of seasonal flowers. Whatever it is, they always do something special on Sunday, as a family.

TWO DOCTORS

There are three hospitals in Baoding called Number One, Two and Three, in no particular order of excellence. In the Number One hospital, there are over 50 doctors. The fundamental division is between those who practice Western medicine and those who use traditional Chinese medicine to treat their patients. Some patients make the choice themselves, reporting to the Chinese medicine clinic directly for consultation. Others take the advice of the doctor who examines them and accept either Chinese or Western medicine or a combination of the two. As there are no "general practitioners" in China, all medicine is practised in clinics or hospitals, with both types of medicine being available.

The main difference between Chinese and Western medicine is that the former relies on traditional herbal remedies listed in ancient textbooks, and on acupuncture. Western medicine uses drugs prepared in chemical factories and the sort of surgery that we all know. It is common

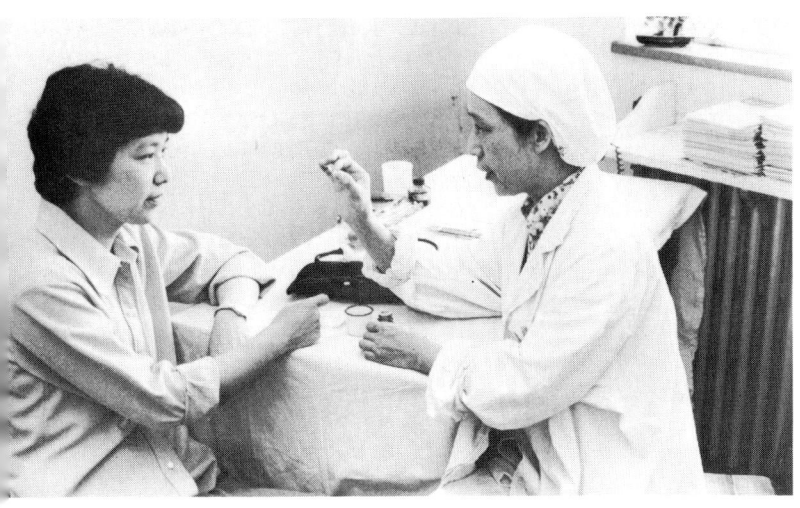

A Western-style doctor explains the correct use of medicines. Medical treatment is free for state-employed workers and their families. The workers in co-operative or private ventures have to pay for treatment and medicines, as do peasants.

A prescription is measured out in a traditional Chinese pharmacy. Wonderful smells come from the small drawers which contain dried herbs, roots, flower-petals and fruit-peel. The pharmacist is using a steel yard, still in common use in China as a weighing instrument.

in China for Western medicine to be used for acute cases and for those which obviously require surgery, whilst Chinese medicine is used for long-term, chronic illnesses like rheumatism, arthritis, stomach or back problems and migraine. Acupuncture, where fine needles are inserted into different acu-points all over the body, is used to control pain. It cannot cure disease but it can alleviate pain and related symptoms. When herbal remedies are prescribed patients are given little parcels of different herbs, ranging from dried orange peel to rare roots, which they boil with water to make medicinal soups.

Dr Liang, a woman in her fifties, was trained in Western medicine and surgery in Peking and has been working in Baoding for over 20 years. At first, her family life was difficult as her husband, an eye specialist, was still working in Peking and they could not often afford to buy a ticket for the three-hour train ride from Baoding to Peking. Dr Liang lived with her mother, who looked after her two girls, and her husband came to stay four or five times a year.

After ten years of this separation her husband finally managed to get a transfer to the hospital at Baoding when the eye surgeon there retired. Dr Liang's mother continued to look after the children until her death, by which time they were old enough to come home from school alone and help with the supper.

Dr Liang runs one of the clinics in the hospital where patients first come for a consultation, so her job is very much like that of a general practitioner. She notes the case history, makes her diagnosis and then discusses the best line of treatment with the patient. She frequently asks Dr Liu to help with treatment. Dr Liu is a Chinese medicine specialist who trained at Baoding hospital. He is a senior doctor and his tasks include the supervision of a herb garden where some of the medicinal herbs required are grown. He spends much of his spare time travelling out into the countryside in search of more herbs and roots, which are dried and chopped in his dispensary. Dr Liu's wife is a dispenser. She takes the prescriptions and then weighs out the right amounts of peppermint leaves, mushrooms and dried bark, bundling them in brown paper and copying out the instructions as to how they should be boiled and used. She rolls some powdered medicines up in a paste, forming large soft balls which, again, have to be dissolved in hot water and drunk like tea.

Dr Liu and Dr Liang discuss the best

way of treating their patients. Quite often they use a combination of techniques. Chinese herbal teas and acupuncture are often used, for example, to relieve pain and other problems after major Western-style surgery, and acupuncture alone may be used instead of a Western anaesthetic for minor surgery. Dr Liang's husband does quite a lot of eye operations with acupuncture analgesia. When acupuncture is used to remove the pain of surgery the patient is fully conscious and so he or she can usually walk away from the operating theatre immediately, and recovery is much quicker. The equipment required is far simpler and cheaper than the paraphernalia of a Western operating theatre, and the cheapness of the whole operation is important in a poor country like China.

A doctor's pay is low, although Dr Liang's husband, as a surgeon of national importance, earns more than his wife. Dr Liang herself doesn't earn much more than a school teacher, which means that she cannot afford to pay for help with cleaning and cooking at home but has to do all the chores herself. She goes to bed at almost midnight and gets up at 6.30 a.m. to prepare rice gruel for the family breakfast and tidy the house before bicycling off to the hospital at 7.40 a.m. Her patients are already queuing up when she arrives at the clinic in time for the 8 o'clock start. She works straight through, without a minute even to glance at the clock, until 11.30 a.m., when she goes to lunch in the canteen. Her children, who attend the local technical college and teacher training college also eat there in their break, and sometimes she sees them for a few minutes at lunch time before she rushes off to visit some of her patients in the wards. Then it's back to the clinic to see more patients at 2.30 p.m. Dr Liang's working day ends at 5 o'clock, when she bicycles home past the market to try and pick up some fresh vegetables and a small piece of pork or a chicken for supper.

Her children help to wash and chop the vegetables and lay the table for supper. Their studies have to be interrupted by supper as the only table in the small flat serves as both desk and dining-table. When the supper dishes have been washed up, the children continue with their books and essays while Dr Liang mends the family's clothes. The children go to bed in the only other room in the flat (where their father sits and reads for a bit of peace and quiet whilst supper is being prepared and homework done), leaving the larger room to their parents. Dr Liang's husband continues to read his books on optical surgery whilst Dr Liang herself sits on the bed surrounded by medical journals. She tries to find time every evening to do a bit of reading to keep up with the latest medical advances, but often falls asleep over her journals and books.

Because Dr Liang's husband was a famous eye surgeon, who specialized in complex operations of a rarified sort, he was banned from surgery for several years during the Cultural Revolution. As part of the attack on privilege and individual prestige there was a movement to take medicine out into the countryside, where peasants had primitive facilities, if any. Specialists were accused of treating only a few rich city patients instead of putting their skills to the service of the masses. Dr Liang's husband was forced to work as a porter in the hospital mortuary as a form of punishment. He was often sent out on exhausting trips to treat common eye disorders in distant and remote mountain villages, trekking on foot over mountain ranges with a heavy medical case on his back. He was paid very little all that time, but his back pay was returned to him after 1976 and this now forms the basis of their bank account of several thousand *yuan*.

Although Dr Liang and her husband

don't earn a great deal they have been able to add to their savings because they have so little time to go out shopping or to the theatre or cinema. They are planning to buy a colour television because they feel their children are missing out, although Dr Liang is worried about the conflict with their studies. They could spend all their money on a Japanese television set, which many people aspire to, but Dr Liang is firmly against it, not just because it would cost so much but because her family suffered terribly in the war against Japan (1937-1945). Her father was arrested by the Japanese invaders in Peking and died in prison, and her mother had to beg for a while to support herself and her two girls before they managed to walk to Tianjin, where an uncle took them in. Although she was only nine when her father died, Dr Liang remembers the terrifying time very clearly and will have nothing to do with anything Japanese even now, over 40 years later. She often says to her husband that it is a good thing the Americans and Europeans lead in her field of Western medicine; if it was the Japanese she would have to change to something else.

Dr Liu's family live in the next block of flats, in the housing estate that belongs to the hospital, and he occasionally calls on Dr Liang in the evening to discuss the treatment of a particular case. Both doctors find they are so busy during the day that it is only in the evenings, away from the hospital, that they can discuss a case in detail. Whilst Dr Liang and her husband often feel that not enough money is spent on equipment in the hospital (Dr Liang's husband is very jealous of the laser that his old hospital in Peking has bought for eye surgery), and that China lags behind the West in consequence, Dr Liu is full of optimism. In the journals that he reads in the evenings there is constant reference to a growing interest in traditional medicines and acupuncture in the West. There is such a vast amount of literature on traditional medicine in China, and so much experimentation to be done to see which old medicines are really effective — like Chinese lavender for breast cancer, "wood-ear" fungus for stomach cancer and acupuncture for the relief of untreatable pain — that his only regret is that he is so busy he doesn't have time for many experiments himself.

THE TEACHER

Mrs Zhang Ming is 40 and has been teaching in a village primary school for nearly 20 years. She is married to an accountant who works for the commune administration. They have two children, a boy of 12 and a girl of 8. Like all trained professionals the Zhangs work for the State. Their wages are fixed as part of a national salary scale and the average wage is 60 *yuan* a month (about £20).

They live in a typical North Chinese village house surrounded by a high wall. Inside the wall is a low, single-storey building of three rooms. It is raised above ground level on a stone platform and above the waist-high walls is a double row of windows made of wooden lattice which creates a pretty geometric pattern.

Besides the main wing of the house there is a small brick building, where Mrs Zhang does the cooking, and a combined pigsty, hen-house and lavatory — the hens live above the pigs, who live back-to-back with the lavatory. All the manure, both human and animal, is swept out regularly and later used to fertilize the Zhang's vegetable plot. There are two apricot trees in the wide, neatly swept courtyard and a vine, which is cut down and covered in straw to protect it in winter but which, in summer,

Primary school children in Xiamen. School equipment is still simple and discipline is strict. City children tend to get better equipment and teaching, while in the country it is common for children to miss school at busy agricultural times such as harvest.

grows all over a trellis to provide a patch of shade. Water comes from a well in the courtyard.

The Zhang family get up before six, wash their faces in cold water and clean their teeth before breakfast – a simple meal of rice gruel flavoured with home-made pickled vegetables. The children help to feed the hens and the pigs before going off to school with their mother, where classes start at 8 o'clock. Mrs Zhang teaches 40 children between the ages of seven and nine. The classroom is simply furnished with desks in neat rows, a blackboard, an old harmonium which is very out of tune, and the childrens' paintings are pinned to the wall. She teaches Reading and Writing, Mathematics, simple Science, History and Geography, Politics and Physical Education. The most important task for the children is to learn to read and write. They have to master a couple of thousand different Chinese characters before they leave primary school at 12. Activities like painting, singing and dancing all play their part in learning to master the complicated characters, some of which have over 20 separate strokes that have to be written in the right order. Dancing helps to improve physical co-ordination; learning the words of songs helps to train the memory; and painting, often copying, helps to improve control of the brush that is used in Chinese writing.

At 11.30 there is a two-hour break when the children go home for lunch, and Mrs Zhang takes her two children back home. She prepares rice and two simple dishes of vegetables, sometimes with a little meat, and her husband joins the family for lunch. In the afternoon, Mrs Zhang goes back to school, where lessons continue until 4 p.m. She stays on until about 5 o'clock, supervising the football games and after-school activities that

Children playing ping-pong in Shanghai. Outside many blocks of flats brick and concrete ping-pong tables are built for children to play on after school.

occupy the children while their parents are still working in the fields.

When she arrives home Mrs Zhang makes supper — the same sort of simple meal as lunch, perhaps including an omelette made from her own hen's eggs. Her husband sits close to the single electric light, reading books about accounting, Mrs Zhang sews and mends the family's clothes and the children do their homework. In the summer, the children sleep in the right-hand room, on the brick platform that serves as a bed, and the parents sleep on the brick platform in the left-hand room. During the cold winter they light a little stove of charcoal and push it under the brick platform in the left-hand room and the whole family sleeps on the brick platform, warmed from below by the glowing charcoal.

Mrs Zhang considers that she was lucky. She comes from a local peasant family but was clever enough to go to middle school in the nearby town and then to teacher training college in Tianjin, 20 miles away from her home village. She started there in 1963 and during her last year at college the Cultural Revolution broke out. Studies were interrupted as the students formed themselves into Red Guard Detachments and walked out into the countryside to tell the peasants about the Cultural Revolution. Mrs Zhang, who was, and still is, quiet and shy, did not take part in the political meetings but went into peasant houses and helped the peasants write letters and do their accounts.

When she was 24, Mrs Zhang started "going out" with her husband, whom she had known since they were children. They married the following year.

"There have been a lot of changes recently. Now that the peasants work for themselves, they sometimes keep the children at home in the busy times, to help in the fields. I go to their homes and explain that they mustn't interrupt the children's schooling. It is important to learn so that they can help their parents later. If they can read and write and do maths, they can help to run the family's affairs. It is difficult to make them see that sometimes; they are interested in making money now, not thinking about the future. But it is part of my job to make them think about the future."

On Sundays, when the school is closed, Mrs Zhang does the washing, using cold water from the well and hanging the clothes out to dry in the courtyard. Her husband works hard in their vegetable plot and he sometimes stops there on his way home from work during the week, too.

"We have quite a lot of money if you take our two salaries together, but we don't have the same opportunities as the peasants to make extra money. Our salaries are fixed by the State and they don't go up much. We have plenty of food and we have saved up to buy a black and white television because we think it is important for our children's education. I would like them to be able to go to university but there is such competition for places nowadays. I don't know if they stand a chance, coming from a village like this. I try and encourage them to work hard and to do extra work in the evenings but they don't have the advantages of city children."

SERVICE INDUSTRIES

Shoppers fighting their way through a department store in Guangzhou (Canton). People have quite a bit of money these days, with bonuses and compensation for injuries during the Cultural Revolution, but there are not enough new, desirable goods to go round, so shops are full.

As a poor country, China has a far greater range of service industries than can be found in the wealthier, more industrialized West. It is possible to have all sorts of things repaired which would perhaps be thrown away in the West: plimsolls, cheap fountain pens, cheap watches, electrical goods, saucepans and enamel basins. For the Chinese, with rising prices to contend with, it is not easy to replace such items, so they are taken for repair, either to Government-run shops or to the numerous new privately run roadside stalls. Any street market in China, besides providing food of all sorts, has rows of repairers, streetside haircutters and barbers, and tailors with sewing machines ready to patch worn clothes or run up cheap copies of fashionable Western suits, made to measure. Almost all the street markets are supervised, with licensed stalls for which the stall-holder pays a very small sum plus a percentage of earnings over a fixed amount. Inspectors patrol the markets looking for unlicensed traders or people who come in with, perhaps, ten pairs of shoes to sell. Food is also inspected to make sure that it is fit to sell and that stall-holders, especially those selling meat, maintain a reasonable standard of hygiene. As the Chinese prefer to buy live hens, ducks and fish, these are certain to be fresh, but pork and beef are sold in ready-cut joints and these have to be inspected.

Some service industries have existed for a long time: restaurants and hotels are often proud of their history, and some shops can also trace their origins back a few hundred years, even if they are now state run. The standard of service varies. Large department stores in the major cities are always crowded with shoppers, and the assistants may be overworked and short-tempered. Since 1976 a small number of new hotels in major cities have been built and run as "joint ventures", financed and managed by foreigners, for foreign visitors. These have set high standards of service, in an attempt to match any international hotel. Staff are trained to provide prompt and efficient service and are rewarded with bonuses, like factory workers. By contrast, in some State-run hotels the staff have discovered that life is easier if it is spent sitting about, chatting or reading rather than looking after guests, and sometimes it seems as if they are trying to frighten visitors away. Managers of both shops and hotels try and exhort their staff to be more pleasant and welcoming.

Shop managers, in particular, need to encourage trade – there is growing competition from privately owned shops which, unsubsidized by the Government, try to attract buyers by offering better and more willing service. The same is true of restaurants. There are still not enough restaurants in China to accommodate everyone who wants or needs to eat out, and the last few years have seen a great expansion of privately run restaurants where special efforts are made to attract clients.

A new industry that is beginning to expand in China is that of tourism. Tourists from abroad have been coming in ever-increasing numbers since the early 1970s. In 1985, 18 million visitors arrived from abroad. Over 90% of these were "Overseas Chinese" from Hong Kong, but 420,000 were from nearby Japan and 225,000 from the United States. These last – and visitors from Europe, Australia and other parts of the world – require guides from the China Travel Service, and specially built hotels, fleets of minibuses and aeroplanes to get around. They contribute enormously to China's foreign currency reserves by spending, on average, some £750 per person in China itself, and often travelling on China's international airline. The effect of tourism on China is complex: many tourist sites are now full of peasants selling souvenirs; hotels with the sorts of luxuries foreigners expect are being built at a tremendous rate; temples, museums and other sites receive revenue to pay for upkeep from both the Government and from ticket sales; peasants can find extra labouring work in the winter months widening roads near popular tourist sites which are clogging up with extra

English language students in Shenzhen. Though they are living in a dormitory, they are dressed in the latest fashions. Cafés, popular with the young, are full of girls in silvery evening dresses, an odd contrast with the sombre clothes of older people. After graduating from language school, these girls will work as interpreters, either for business concerns or for tourists.

The tourist industry creates a network of subsidiary industries. In this workshop outside Xi'an, one of the most popular tourist cities since the discovery of the "terracotta army", women make models of terracotta soldiers and a seventh-century pagoda, another local landmark. The souvenirs are sold all over town.

traffic. Thus direct and indirect profits are numerous.

It is not only foreigners who want to travel in China: since 1976 an enormous number of Chinese tourists are discovering their own country. In Shanghai, tourist agencies have opened, offering local residents conducted tours to the capital or to the buried army at Xi'an or to the beautiful Buddhist island of Putuo, just off the coast south of Shanghai. The tours are organized Japanese-style, every tourist being provided with an identical cap in blue and white and the tour-leader urging them on with a whistle. The growth in internal tourism helps to put an additional strain on the number of hotel rooms, airline seats and places on trains, though it does stimulate the development of subsidiary service industries.

THE TOURIST GUIDE

The first person that any foreigner meets on entering China is the woman who collects health certificates. The second is the immigration official, who stamps passports, and the third is by far the most important: the interpreter or guide.

Xiao Lu has been working for the Government-run China Travel Service for two years. She studied English at the Foreign Languages Institute in Xi'an and after graduating was assigned to work as a tourist guide, based in Xi'an. Now 23, she is just about used to her work and is no longer afraid of the tourist groups she has to look after.

Xiao Lu doesn't work a regular six-day week like office workers. She looks after, perhaps, seven groups a month, usually for three days, and when she has seen one group on to the train or the plane (and waited until the plane actually takes off), she has a day or two's holiday before going off to the station or airport to meet the next group of English-speaking tourists. Once or twice a year she is sent to Peking or Canton to meet a group as they enter the country. She then travels around China with them for a couple of weeks, making such arrangements as are necessary in conjunction with the local guides. Xiao Lu still enjoys these trips as she gets to see other parts of China and, more importantly, gets to do some shopping. Many highly prized items are much cheaper in the areas in which they are produced than they are in Xi'an: oranges of all sorts from Sichuan, tiny tangerines from Jiangsu; special volcanic rocks for making miniature gardens from mountain areas; herbal medicines and tonics, like the *tian ma* root and a special bruise ointment, from Yunnan; new fashions in clothes from Shanghai and Canton. Xiao Lu doesn't only buy for herself: she takes orders from friends and family and always comes back laden down after one of her trips.

One advantage of contact with foreigners is that they sometimes give tips — either the special "foreign currency coupons" or items of clothing, books and the like. The coupons can be used to buy imported electrical goods, personal stereos, neat and efficient cameras from Japan and cosmetics from France and America. They can also be sold (illegally) for twice or three times their face value. Most people in China covet Japanese electrical items but if they buy them in ordinary currency the Government import tax makes them very expensive, sometimes as much as four times the foreign currency coupon price. But the coupons are not easy to get hold of, hence their black-market price.

Xiao Lu thinks tourists are all rich and extravagant.

"They throw away perfectly good things, just because their suitcases are too full. And they buy such a lot here. Some of them spend thousands of *yuan* on carpets made of silk or huge paintings, and they don't even bat an eyelid. We take them to a lot of shops, to encourage them to spend their money, because that way the country gets more foreign exchange."

Most people spend two or three days in Xi'an. The main tourist attraction is the "buried army", a huge pit containing about 7000 life-size soldiers and horses, all made of clay, dressed in clay armour and drawn up in battle order. Another popular

Old ladies burning incense in a Buddhist temple in Chengdu. Buddhism, like Christianity, Islam and Taoism, is officially tolerated partly because it helps to bring tourists to beautiful, historic temples. The government supports such temples, providing money to rebuild and repaint and also salaries for one or two monks to work as caretakers. Other monks are supported by believers, who pay them to hold services.

Foreign tourists on the Great Wall near Peking.

tourist spot is the Hot Springs Park near Xi'an. Because there are so many tourists in Xi'an careful planning is needed. The Travel Service office divides them into two groups: one group goes to the "buried army" in the morning, the other in the afternoon, alternating with the hot springs. There are two places near the hot springs where the tourists can have lunch, so, Xiao Lu says, they just about manage, though people do say it is like rush-hour.

Other places to visit in Xi'an are the museum, local handicraft factories, where visitors can do more shopping, or the mosque. There are over 40,000 Muslims in Xi'an and the mosque, built in the Chinese style, is over 1000 years old.

Xiao Lu's job is a fairly tiring one, for when she is looking after a group she usually has to stay with them 24 hours a day. The dormitory provided by the Government is not near any of the hotels frequented by foreigners, so she moves into the hotel with them. There, at least she has plenteous supplies of hot water — in the dormitory she has to share a room with five other unmarried girls who work for the travel service and they only have hot water for showers twice a week. If the group's national guide (who travels with them all over China) is a man Xiao Lu may well get a hotel room to herself, but she has to share if the national guide is a woman.

"My pay is very low as I have only just started work but there are plenty of perks in this job. Apart from tips and gifts and things that tourists give away, if I arrange for them to have a meal out I get to eat for free and can keep my daily food money. I save money by buying things cheaply when I go travelling and I get better things that way. It is hard work, but a lot of people work much harder than me for less. It was difficult at first when I couldn't really understand what the foreigners meant, but I am used to them now. They all ask the same questions anyway."

THE ELDERLY WAITER AND HIS WIFE

Mr Tan is in his seventies and works in the newly re-opened "Coffee Shop" in one of Shanghai's most famous hotels. He speaks perfect, if old-fashioned, English and a little French and German (a few useful phrases only). He began at the hotel in 1925 and has worked there ever since.

Though he is past retiring age he is kept on because he knows how to wait at table, knows the right things to say, and knows how a good old-fashioned hotel should be run. The younger waiters don't pay much attention to detail.

"They wear dirty jackets, they spill food on the table-cloths, they lounge about and don't notice when guests are trying to attract their attention, they don't bother to learn foreign languages so that they can help foreign guests — I don't understand them at all. I like to feel that I do my job well, that people will go away satisfied with discreet but attentive service, but the young people don't care at all. All they think about is their pay-packet and doing as little as possible to earn it."

Mr Tan works in the afternoons and evenings, opening the coffee shop at 3 p.m. and staying there until 10.30 p.m. when, after washing up and clearing the tables, he bicycles slowly home through the dark streets. He and his wife live in one room in an old house in what used to be the French Quarter before the war, when Shanghai was divided up between various foreign powers. The house looks just like any French suburban house, with a red-tiled roof and elegant iron gates, but the washing hanging from the windows on bamboo poles give it a slightly untidy look. Mrs Tan worked as housekeeper to a British banker living in Shanghai until she retired, ten years ago. Before 1949 she had worked for the same bank, as a maid in the manager's house, a job which she continued to do through all the political upheavals of the 1950s and after.

Mrs Tan was born into a country family in a village not far from Shanghai. Her family wasn't one of the poorest in the village and they were able to afford to bind her feet. This meant that they lost her as an effective worker in the fields, but they hoped she would one day be able to get a job in the city. Mrs Tan's cousin worked in the residence of the Assistant Manager of a large bank in Shanghai and when Mrs Tan was 14 her cousin managed to find her a job as under-housemaid to the Manager.

Everything in the house was strange, from the house itself, built on two floors unlike the one-storeyed, thatched farmhouse with a dirt floor that she was used to, to the white woman who lived in it, with her big feet and apparently bare legs. The young girl soon learned how to wax floors, polish silver and dust ornaments. She often felt homesick but gradually came to like life "below stairs" with the other servants and their families and friends, who had quite a social life in the kitchen and out-house. She learned pidgin English so that she could understand orders — "Master want cocktail? Bring chop-chop [quickly]" — and tripped around the house quite cheerfully.

Mrs Tan met her husband a few years after she came to Shanghai. He worked as a waiter in one of Shanghai's big hotels. Traditional weddings in China were expensive affairs, because the bride was supposed to bring a dowry and the bridegroom was expected to send expensive presents to the bride's family. Neither Mr or Mrs Tan's families could afford these expenses, but they decided to get married anyway.

Soon afterwards, the Japanese occupied Shanghai. Mrs Tan's employer's wife and children left Shanghai soon after, never to return, for the Japanese were threatening to intern all foreigners. This they eventually did, and the Bank Manager himself spent over a year in a Japanese prison camp, very close to his handsome house. When the Japanese came to take him away the servants fled from the well-known brutality of the soldiers. Mrs Tan rushed, as fast as she could on her bound feet, to the hotel to wait until her husband came off duty. He had a bed in a dormitory in the hotel but as

Three families now live in this old courtyard house where once a single family would have occupied the entire courtyard. Though people maintain the interior quite well there is an acute shortage of paint in China, so the exterior of buildings is often quite shabby.

she couldn't stay there they found a tenement, where they shared one room divided by a curtain with another cousin of Mr Tan's and his wife and their small baby.

Mr Tan's hotel did not close during the Japanese occupation, as it was filled with Japanese military officers and businessmen. All went reasonably well for the Tans until Mrs Tan was injured in a bombing raid. They had to spend all their meagre savings on hospital treatment and still blame their lack of children on her injuries.

When the Japanese left Shanghai after their defeat in the Second World War Mr Tan continued to work in the hotel, whilst Mrs Tan went back to see the new manager of the bank, who had returned to take up business. She was offered a job as housekeeper and remained there until she retired. The only change for her came in 1949 when the new State took over the provision of domestic staff for foreign diplomats and businessmen. She became an employee of the Service Bureau, receiving her wages from the Bureau rather than the bank, and was required to write a weekly report on events in the household. The Service Bureau charged a great deal for servants (though it only paid them a fraction of the amount it received), and though the foreigners were therefore keen to reduce their staff to a minimum they insisted on the maintenance of a certain number. Mrs Tan worked every day as cleaner and cook, with an elderly man who served at table, opened the door to visitors and served cocktails to their solitary employer. He was often away visiting his family in Hong Kong, so the work was not hard. After making his supper and washing up, Mrs Tan took the bus home at 9 p.m.

The Tans worry now that they are old and have no children to look after them. They won't need to go into the rare old people's homes in China as they have many relatives and could stay with them if life on their own gets too hard. They won't be completely unwelcome as they will have their pensions as State employees. Pensions are usually 80% of the normal salary and will help to contribute to their care. But they know that it is not easy suddenly to enter a new household full of young people with their own lives to lead, and they hope that it won't be necessary. They have heard stories of elderly people being ill-treated by their young relatives, and they do not want to become a burden.

A retired man playing *weiqi* (Japanese "go") in a Shanghai park. Life for the elderly in China is quite organized. Parks are full of games like this and in the tea-houses the elderly are entertained by singers, story-tellers and musicians. It is difficult to be lonely in crowded, sociable China.

TWO SELF-EMPLOYED BOYS

Wu Weiguo and his friend Sun Ping sit side by side on the pavement near a main road in Wuhan. They are both 17 and left school last year but there were no jobs for them. Rather than sit at home all day they decided that they would set up repair stalls, Weiguo repairing bicycles and Ping doing shoe repairs. The local neighbourhood committee approved their scheme, suggested a spot that they could occupy and helped Ping by providing him with an old machine for sewing leather. Both of them have permits to obtain scrap rubber, which Ping uses for soling shoes and Weiguo, who gets worn-out inner-tubes, uses for repairing punctures. The prices they charge are fixed officially by the State. A simple puncture costs 20 cents and there is a sliding scale from 20 cents to 1 *yuan* for shoe repairs, depending on what needs doing.

Boys on the beach at Xiamen. Leisure is increasingly important in China, partly because of unemployment, but also because life has been hard for so long that people now want a bit of luxury. Unfortunately, the population is so great that there are not enough facilities to provide for all, and therefore there is only one day off a week for workers and no holidays, except for national holidays (like Bank holidays).

Rather than sit around at home many unemployed people set up repair stalls on the roadside.

They both quite enjoy their work, on sunny days at least. On rainy days, in a huge, green-hooded mackintosh, Weiguo sometimes goes and sits on his little stool, because bicycles still break down and get punctures in the rain (and their grateful riders very occasionally give him an extra 10 cents), but Ping usually stays at home, because people don't want to stand in the rain waiting for their shoes to be stitched up. He quite often has a few neighbours' shoes to repair at home.

They live almost next door to each other in a small lane near their site and walk to work together at about 8 o'clock. They have lunch together, usually a bowl of noodles with aniseed-flavoured meat soup, served by a girl who runs a noodle stall on the street corner. Ping says:

"We don't make much money. For both of us its about the same, maybe five yuan a week on average, which isn't much, but then we still live at home so we don't have to pay rent. I don't know that I'd like to do this for years, but it is better than sitting at home. We were best friends at school so its nice to be able to work together, or side by side anyway."

Wu Weiguo adds:

"We are both still registered for jobs, and I'd like to have a proper salary. But I think I might be more choosy now. At least I'm my own master and I can work as hard as I like or take a day off without getting into trouble. I don't think I'd take just any job now."

Wu Weiguo and Sun Ping are perhaps unusual because they quite like what they do and don't think it is demeaning to do a service job from the roadside.

"Quite a few of our school-friends think we're mad. They haven't got jobs but they say they wouldn't be seen dead by the side of the road. Some of them are really cynical. They don't see any hope here and they'd rather go to Shanghai or, better still, abroad. If you haven't got relatives abroad then you don't have a chance of leaving China so why bother to think about it?

They're the ones who get into trouble. There are always campaigns to tidy up young people, stop them wearing jewellery or making them shave off their moustaches and cut their hair. If you do something, then people take less notice of you because at least you are trying to earn a living."

Neither Weiguo nor Ping is interested in politics and, though they were both members of the Young Pioneers at school, neither has any desire to join the Communist Party. Weiguo says he's a realist:

"I don't expect the Party would have me anyway. You have to be in a proper job and heading for the top, not mending bicycles. Anyway, I'd rather go to the cinema than to a political meeting."

TRANSPORTATION

Some of China's great early achievements lay in the development of ships and canals. The Grand Canal, linking the rich rice-fields of the Yangtse delta with the cold capital of Peking, was begun under the Sui dynasty (A.D. 581-618), and a navigational compass for use on sea-going boats was first developed in China. Waterways and rivers were commonly used for transportation, even when they were difficult and dangerous, as were the Yangtse gorges before a dam was built ten years ago and the treacherous Yellow River, popularly known as "China's sorrow". It got this name because the huge amount of silt it carries raises the bed above the surrounding countryside and has caused several drastic changes of course, deluging huge tracts of land and destroying everything in its path. Though the river is now protected by dykes the silt still pours down, continuing to raise the bed to dangerous levels.

In the nineteenth century, railways were built, mostly by foreigners, in various parts of China. This has led to some problems as the gauges they used were not always the same width. The French, for example, whose "sphere of interest" was the south-western province of Yunnan and neighbouring Vietnam, built a railway linking the two and, even today, passengers wishing to go from Peking towards Vietnam have to change trains. Though more miles of railway line have been built since 1949, many of the lines are single-track and simply cannot cope with the volume of traffic. Most recently, road-building, which is cheaper, has overtaken railway-building, in an attempt to relieve China's transport congestion, but problems still remain. Many of the older roads are badly surfaced and all of them are now too narrow to take the volume of traffic. Considerable jams occur if there are accidents, or at points where long-distance lorry-drivers stop for lunch on narrow roads.

Part of the traffic problem lies in the variety of vehicles on the roads. There are horse, mule and bullock carts moving slowly; hand-held tractors, converted into carts, moving only slightly faster; overloaded public buses, with ducks on the roof, pulling in and out from bus-stops; huge lorries (often Japanese-made) tearing along; cars, with curtained windows concealing army generals, overtaking everything; and thousands of bicycles, often supporting heavy loads.

In the cities, too, the number of bicycles complicates the traffic flow. Though bicycle lanes have been fenced off on the wider roads, on side streets, overcrowded buses, lorries and taxis compete for space between cyclists. City cyclists are not allowed to carry passengers, nor to ride holding open umbrellas but, though they face on-the-spot fines from traffic police, they don't seem to care. In Peking, with a population of about 9 million, there are said to be 6 million bicycles.

As more and more Chinese travel, either on business or for pleasure, pressure on transportation grows. The provision of more and better transport facilities (along with better energy supplies) is now seen as a major priority for China, not only to improve industrial output, but also to make life easier for the luckless travellers. Many poorer people travel by long-distance buses, which are slow and terribly uncomfortable, as the seats are worn out on the older buses; others fight their way on to trains. There are four types of seat on long-distance trains: soft sleeper (four-berth), soft seat, hard sleeper (where the entire carriage is fitted with rows of wooden slatted bunks in tiers of three) and hard seat. Because of the single track and lack of rolling-stock, there are not very many trains to choose from – perhaps one or two per day – so all are permanently full and some are much slower than others.

For foreign tourists who, together with important Chinese bureaucrats or army officials, travel in soft sleepers a train trip is, however, always a pleasure. The trains travel slowly, allowing a good view of the countryside; freshly cooked food in the dining car (liberally decorated with pretty plants in porcelain pots) is delicious; and each compartment is supplied with porcelain tea-mugs and a thermos of hot water.

Pedestrian walkways in Shanghai. Below, the pavement is closed off by a railing to prevent people crossing where they please. One of the world's most populous cities, Shanghai is very congested. It is an interesting city, with its mixture of Western and Chinese architecture.

A child in a bicycle cart. Many goods are taken to market in bicycle carts like these. The child waits for his father to take him home.

A horse-drawn bus in Yunnan. Owing to the shortage of transport facilities, all sorts of animals and carts are used. Outside Kunming, the capital of Yunnan, horse buses are common, seating approximately ten people.

Illegal bicycle transport. While it is not uncommon to see an entire family on a bicycle, for safety reasons it is illegal, and this family could be subject to an on-the-spot fine. Racing bicycles with lighter frames are beginning to become popular in China but a family like this is better off with a solid, heavy machine.

A long-distance bus stuck in a traffic jam. Public buses link all major towns and villages, covering some 200-300 km in a day at the most, though a few overnight buses stop less often and cover greater distances.

Rush-hour in Peking, dominated by bicycles. The bicycle lane is separated from other traffic by a solid barrier.

BOAT PEOPLE

The Zheng family live in the small town of Wan Xian, perched high above the Yangtse at the head of the dangerous narrow gorges that have always made the Yangtse a treacherous, though necessary, waterway. The river connects the fertile province of Sichuan, a rich vegetable-growing area (also famous for its brocades, lacquer wares and bamboo), with the coastal province of Zhejiang and the great port of Shanghai.

Mr Zheng works on a small steamer, *Red Flag No. 285*, which travels up and down the river, hauling cargo. Larger steamers travel the length of the river, taking five days to reach Shanghai downstream and seven to get back against the current, but Mr Zheng's boat usually only travels up to the stone quarries and then down to the

Small coastal steamers in the port of Xiamen. Coastal boat traffic is a common form of transport both for people and for goods. Larger steamers also cruise up and down the coast.

Gezhouba dam, on the other side of the gorges. He is rarely away from home more than one night.

The first steamers came up the river in the nineteenth century, but sail remained the most common method of transport for many decades afterwards. Before the dam raised the level of the water in the gorges, there were many treacherous rocks and shoals that had to be avoided, and one of the advantages of the shallow sailing boats was that they could pass at almost all times of the year. Steam boats, which sat deeper in the water, could only pass through the dangerous gorges in spring and summer when rain raised the level of the water.

It wasn't possible for sailing boats to get upstream through the gorges unless they were hauled manually against the flood by trackers, who would wait in their teams of 12 at Yichang, near where the Gezhouba dam is being completed. The trackers' paths, carved out of the stone high up can still be seen above the water when it is not in flood. Mr Zheng's father was a tracker and he can remember his father's heavily calloused shoulder, marked by the ropes that were used to haul the boats.

The dam, which is still not finished, has raised the level of the Yangtse and has been fairly effective in controlling the disastrous floods that used to sweep down the river every summer after the rains. The water level still rises by many feet in the late summer and Mr Zheng is used to seeing drowned pigs and cats floating by on the reddish water at that time of the year. In some bad years, when the floods up-river in Sichuan are particularly heavy, he occasionally sees human corpses being swept by.

In late summer the Yangtse flows high and very fast. To moor at a landing stage requires considerable skill and quick reactions. The large steamers that carry hundreds of passengers up and down the river have to lay an anchor chain across the river and slowly feed it through the boat in order to moor. If the captain didn't use the anchor chain he would either destroy the landing stage by hitting it at speed or he might miss it completely as the river raced him downstream. Mr Zheng's small steamer is easier to manoeuvre but it still requires considerable experience of the different water conditions.

Though much of the cargo is made up of stones from local quarries, there are seasonal variations. Sichuan is famous for its citrus fruits — oranges, mandarins and huge pomeloes — which are welcomed in markets all over China. In the autumn *Red Flag No. 285* often carries a load of oranges or mandarins down to Yichang, from where it will be shipped further down the Yangtse.

Mr Zheng's wife works as a clerk in the Wan Xian port authority office. She has seen changes recently now that tourist boats have begun to visit the picturesque gorges. As these are still quite difficult for big ships to negotiate, particularly at night, the tourist steamers stop overnight at Wan Xian and set off for the gorges early in the morning.

Most of the tourist boats are large steamers with three floors. Foreign tourists are accommodated at the front of the upper deck, with double cabins and a warm lounge from which they can watch the scenery if clouds and rain descend on the gorges. At the back of the upper deck is a special dining room for foreigners and other important travellers, like army generals and rich businessmen. The rest of the upper deck and the two lower decks are always packed with Chinese travellers, who may only pay a few *yuan* for a space to sleep in for a few nights.

The steamers stop quite frequently and many of the lower deck passengers only go one or two stops, using the boat like a train, as the only way to get along the river. Some, however, travel the whole way to the big cities of Wuhan and Shanghai, way down-river, sleeping beside baskets of fresh ginger or sweet oranges that they will sell in the street markets there for a far higher price than they could get in Sichuan where such things are plentiful.

Mr Zheng is glad of the dam, and of the security of his job compared with that of his father's. He gets a monthly wage, as does his wife, and he works a fairly regular week, only staying away overnight on occasion. His father used to be away for days, sometimes weeks, and the family never knew if he would return or whether he had been swept into the rushing water, for many trackers drowned every year. He died before he was 50, worn out by the heavy work of hauling against the racing river, but Mr Zheng is confident that he will live comfortably and well into his seventies. Some people regret that the dam has raised the water level, because it makes the gorges less exciting and dramatic, but Mr Zheng does not share their feeling. A second dam is being planned, which will further control the river and raise its level within the gorges. If it makes the river easier to deal with Mr Zheng is all in favour of it.

THE BUS DRIVER

Wang Hui drives a number 10 bus across the centre of Peking many times a day. He is 30, married to a shop assistant in a small department store, and has a two-year-old son. He reports for an eight-hour shift six days a week.

"Its a terrible job. I've been driving for ten years now and my salary is still very low. If I'd got a job as a taxi driver I'd have been earning maybe three times as much, not to speak of the extra advantages taxi-drivers get, what with foreign currency and the chance to work for a foreign company. Japanese companies give you electrical goods, radios, tape-recorders and all sorts of things. I don't get anything like that on a bus."

Buses are very crowded in all of China's cities. Recently the city authorities decided to employ a few young people at the most crowded bus stops to push the passengers on to the buses, like the Japanese "pushers" on the Tokyo underground. The "pushers" don't necessarily make the job of a bus driver any easier.

An overcrowded bus in Shanghai. At least the driver is separated from the passengers on this particular bus.

Wang Hui isn't separated from the passengers by any barrier – he doesn't drive from a driver's compartment – so the more people are pushed on to the bus, the more people crowd him and fall over him.

Wang Hui's bus has a conductress on it, a young girl who sits in a seat near the back doors. She is better protected than he is, although she sometimes gets hit in the face by shopping bags as people fight their way on to the bus. She does her best to collect fares, but as there is no way she can struggle through the tightly packed passengers she has to rely on their honesty. She shouts through an intercom system, "Please pass down into the bus, don't crowd the doors, pay your fares now," and some people pass small bundles of notes, from five to 15 cents, along to her and hope to receive a ticket in return. As each stop approaches and Wang Hui slowly steers the bus towards the kerb through banks of slow-moving cyclists, the conductress announces the stop and asks people to make way for those who want to get off. A few passengers, holding their bags high over their heads, squeeze through to the door, and others complain when their feet get stamped on and their bags almost dragged from their hands by the pressure of people moving. The conductress says Wang Hui's route is not as bad as some:

"You may think it is bad here, and it certainly is. There are too many people and too few buses. But if you go to other cities it's the same, or worse. I've seen buses in Luoyang where there are legs sticking out of the windows, people are packed so tight. We got new buses in Peking ten years ago because the Government was embarrassed about the state of public transport when the tourists arrived. But the buses can't take the battering they get and they look worn-out now. Some routes are worse than others. Ours is bad because it passes the main shopping streets and tourist attractions. But the bus out to the Summer Palace from the Zoo is the worst. There are lots of people wanting to go to the Summer Palace but the worst thing is that there has been lots of building along that route. There are thousands of new blocks of flats, stuffed with people, all wanting to get into town or get back home, and few extra buses have been allocated. The bus stops are like mini riots, with people trying to squeeze on to full buses."

When Wang Hui goes home after his eight-hour shift, he is exhausted by the endless battles, the hundreds of people piling on to his bus and squashing him into a corner. He thinks that there ought to be more buses on the routes and that drivers ought to get more money for a difficult job.

THE TAXI DRIVER

Li Jun is a taxi driver for one of the older state-run taxi companies in Peking. He is 25 and has been driving a company cab for two years. He had to pass a stringent driving test, which included written papers, tests in car maintenance and special tests of skill at manoeuvering around obstacles in a test ground.

Many school-leavers would like to become taxi drivers because of the pay and the cachet of driving a car. As there are virtually no private cars in China nobody can learn to drive until they are assigned to a job which involves driving, and the employer teaches the employee. In the last few years private taxi companies have started up in larger cities and they hire drivers from the State-run companies. The expense of car purchase and maintenance is borne by the taxi companies as it would be beyond the means of an individual.

Li Jun works long hours, often ten hours or more a day, but he gets quite a lot of overtime pay and can earn several hundred *yuan* a month if he works really hard. The ability to earn such sums puts taxi drivers in one of

New motorway in Peking. To relieve traffic congestion the Peking government built two further ring roads around the city. While clearly important for transportation many people regret the loss of the character of the old city, which now looks like any modern city anywhere.

the highest income brackets in the capital.

It hasn't always been such a well-paid job. Over the last few years, the methods of payment for taxi drivers have been overhauled several times. Just before Li Jun started work there was a terrific shortage of drivers in the last week of every month. This was because they were on a fixed wage and not allowed to earn any extra. So if they had done enough work to reach that fixed point in the first three weeks of a month they simply wouldn't bother to turn up for work in the last week, leaving angry passengers queuing up for hours outside the major hotels. Now, as Li Jun says, the sky is almost the limit, even if the hours are long.

Li Jun works different shifts but prefers to turn up for work at the usual hour of 8 a.m. He lives in a flat with his parents, close to the taxi company yard where the cars are kept, so he bicycles there every morning. He then starts work. On top of the cab is a yellow sign which lights up when he is free for hire, so taxis can be hailed anywhere on the street. This is a great change. Until recently, taxis were almost exclusively hired by foreigners, businessmen, tourists and diplomats or journalists, but more and more ordinary Chinese now have enough money to take taxis occasionally. Even so, it is always easy to pick up a fare in any of the hotels for foreigners, so Li Jun usually makes his way to a hotel unless he is hailed en route. He would like to improve his Japanese and his English. Then he could offer to put himself at the service of individual clients for the whole of their stay in Peking and would, with luck, pick up a big tip at the end of each visit.

Traffic jams are a relatively new problem. There has been a lot of new road-building in Peking recently: two extra ring roads have been built within the last ten years and the road to the airport, which used to be narrow and jammed with slow-moving mule-carts on their way out to the hills, has been widened. Nevertheless, the main road across town is often solid with traffic and some of the north-south roads, which are narrower, are permanent bottle-necks. Li Jun doesn't take much notice of the traffic: there isn't anything he can do about it and, in a grid city like Peking, there aren't many short-cuts you can take to avoid the jams.

At lunch-time, Li Jun tries to park in the forecourt of the Peking Hotel, near the Forbidden City in the heart of Peking. There is not enough space for all the taxis there, especially since a large number of foreign businessmen live permanently in the hotel and they park their cars there, too. If he can squeeze in he is happy, as the canteen there, for hotel workers and taxi drivers, is cheap and quite good. Not all the hotels provide very good food. After eating meat, rice and vegetables, and having a cigarette with his friends, Li Jun looks to see if there is a queue on the steps, and if there is he may well pick up a fare. If there aren't many people queuing he goes back to his car and sleeps for about three-quarters of an hour.

Li Jun is well aware that he is financially well-off and therefore quite a catch as a husband. He is not entirely happy about the situation, though, for there is one thing that money can't buy – a decent flat. The taxi company is building new apartment blocks for its employees but they won't be finished for a year or two and there is a long waiting list. Li Jun himself is on the lookout for a girl who might have access to good housing. The Chinese often take quite a pragmatic approach to marriage, seeing it as a working union, an attempt to make the most of pooled resources, in a country where resources are shared. People do marry for love, but for many an element of calculation comes into the decision. Li Jun is quite clear about that: if he finds a girl with the right approach to life and access to good housing, he will seriously consider her as a wife – as long as she isn't impossible or hideous. Love will come later; anyway, getting on together is the most important thing and it is difficult to get on well if you are jammed into one room with a child and sharing a kitchen area on a balcony.

Li Jun would like to leave China. He says that all foreigners are rich and have good things – fine suits, leather briefcases, pocket calculators and lots and lots of money (as well as the freedom to move from one country to another). He doesn't imagine he will ever get the chance, although quite a few taxi drivers working out of the "Friendship Hotel" have married foreigners. Foreigners working as teachers or translators for the Chinese Government live in the Friendship Hotel on the outskirts of the city. Li Jun thinks that it could be interesting to marry a foreigner, but there is a lot of red tape involved and, anyway, he hears that some of the marriages don't work out because the husbands can't stand Western food. So he continues to look for a girl who can get a good flat, and his bank account grows steadily, ready for the day when he'll have to buy furniture and fittings for his new home.

ARTS AND CRAFTS

In traditional China, painting and calligraphy were the highest forms of art, and they were practised by all of the educated classes. Scholars who took the imperial exams to become local officials paid almost as much attention to fine calligraphy as they did to the contents of their essays. There were class distinctions in painting, separating the "scholarly" from the "professional" painter. Professional painters often worked in imperial academies, producing bird and flower studies, often using more colour than the scholars, yet the amateur scholar's painting was held in higher esteem. Writing with a brush, painting and composing poetry were inextricably linked. Some of China's greatest poets were also painters of note and, what is more, they worked as scholar-officials in the government service. They administered prefectures, collected taxes and dispensed justice, whilst longing to escape and paint. And on retirement they built themselves tiny gardens in which to sit and enjoy nature.

Today in China there are two major types of painting, still the aristocrat of the arts. Traditional Chinese painting with the soft brush and wash is still taught and practised by many, as is calligraphy, but Western oil painting is also taught in art schools and is increasingly popular. Some of the finest twentieth-century Chinese artists studied abroad and learnt oil techniques before returning to China and often, though not always, to traditional painting.

Sculpture in China, in the past either monumental (religious or funerary) or miniature (tiny jade and ivory carvings for ornament) is heavily influenced by the Western tradition and by Soviet Socialist Realism. In every city centre there is a giant cement sculpture of an improving nature depicting "progress", "peace", "health" or "production".

The performing arts in China show the same range of traditional and Western forms as do the plastic arts. Traditional local opera – a mixture of high-pitched singing, fabulous costume, mime-like gestures and occasional acrobatics – is still popular with older people but is being adapted to new themes. There is a Peking Opera version of Othello and a Southern Opera version of Macbeth, both highly dramatic stories which fit the artificial drama well. Western-style drama is also popular, and plays are written on a variety of social themes, for in China it is the purpose of the arts to instruct and inform. Art must "serve the people", as Mao said, and what he meant was that it should fit in with the Government's socialist ideals. During the Cultural Revolution it was those working in the arts who suffered perhaps most of all, and those who were not in prison or sent away to the remote countryside had to write, produce and act in productions that were savagely censored. For many younger artists, whether painters wishing to paint nudes (not considered proper) or beautiful things

Though times have been very difficult (even after the Cultural Revolution ended in 1976 there have been several campaigns to "clean up" the arts and make them more politically pure) artists now say that they feel freer than they ever have before. The Central Ballet Company of Peking, which had only just begun to perform in the late 1950s, was disbanded in the Cultural Revolution, for ballet was considered a decadent Western art form, but it has recently regrouped and begun to tour the world, presenting both Western classics and new Chinese choreography.

Beside the "high arts" of drama, ballet, painting and sculpture, a tradition of folk art continues to survive in China. Folk arts were also attacked during the Cultural Revolution, accused of being "backward", but they are now being revived, and the arrival of vast numbers of Western tourists is helping that revival. Where families once made items such as kites and tiny stuffed tiger toys, these are now being produced in factory workshops in Shandong; beautiful baskets are woven from bamboo for export; and folk embroidery is produced for sale as souvenirs. Whilst many traditional Chinese products like wooden buckets, bamboo fish-traps, straw

A student rehearsing a Chinese ballet at the Shanghai Dance School.

with no political content, or playwrights wishing to experiment, life is a continual balancing act between censorship and freedom.

Throughout Sichuan province, baskets with lids, decorated with black and red stripes, are made from the plentiful local bamboo. Enterprising peasants board trains loaded down with baskets and take them hundreds of miles to distant markets where they sell well.

sandals and hand-dyed indigo cottons are being replaced by plastic, nylon and polyester, those items likely to survive are the ones that appeal to tourists and craft shops in the West.

THE HANI EMBROIDERER

Not far from the city of Kunming, capital of Yunnan province in south-west China, there is a dramatic limestone formation called the Stone Forest, which consists of millions of limestone columns, formed under the sea nearly 300 million years ago. Covering several square miles, these grey stones, up to 30 metres high, have been carved by rainwater into weird shapes, occasionally embellished by Chinese characters which have been carved on them over the centuries. Visitors come to wander through the "forest" and their tour guides endlessly point out rocks that look like baby water buffaloes half submerged in a pool, like two swans kissing, like lions, or even like Napoleon or George Washington.

Yunnan province, which borders on Vietnam, Burma and Tibet, is not only famous for its limestone: it is also the home of most of China's "minority", or non-Chinese, peoples. Some of these belong to groups which cross borders: Miao people, for example, are found in northern Thailand and some of the Yi live in the neighbouring province of Sichuan. The language, clothing, customs and history of these minority groups are all distinct from each other and from Chinese culture.

Long Mei is a Hani. The Hani minority is related to the Yi (a very large group) and has always lived near the Stone Forest. Their language, connected to the Yi branch of the Tibet-Burman group, is unlike Chinese. In the past they had no writing system, but since 1949 they have learnt to use the Roman alphabet. Children also learn Chinese, both spoken and written, in school. The last published census of 1957 recorded 540,000 Hani people, but as health care has since improved, the numbers must now be higher.

Long Mei is 17, the eldest of five brothers and sisters. The minority peoples may have more than the single child allowed to the Chinese as they are not so numerous and often live in more primitive conditions in distant parts where infant mortality is higher than amongst the Chinese. The Hani are quite privileged in this sense, for they are only about 100 miles away from the provincial capital with its large hospitals.

Long Mei's family is completely dependent on the tourist trade for its income. Her mother, grandmother and her two younger sisters, like hundreds of other women in the village, sit all day over sewing machines, covering bright cotton aprons and bags with strips of embroidered ribbon. The sewing machine has transformed Hani costume, which used to be entirely hand-embroidered, but there are still plenty of women in the village who make little squares of hand embroidery and appliqué work.

It is Long Mei's job to try and sell these locally made goods to the tourists who flock to the Stone Forest. The tourist season is a long one in Yunnan, for the climate on the high plateau is warm and sunny almost all year round. Every day she walks the two miles from the village to the Stone Forest, with the embroideries in a basket strapped to her back. She wears a combination of Chinese and Hani clothes, with a pair of trousers and baseball boots under her pretty, embroidered and beribboned lilac cotton dress and black, embroidered apron.

She stations herself, along with a hundred or so other Hani women, all with roughly the same goods for sale,

A woman of the Hani minority selling embroidery to overseas Chinese visitors at the Stone Forest.

outside the tourist hotel near the Stone Forest. At 7.30 a.m. the first tourists appear, coming to make their last-minute purchases before getting into the tourist buses for the drive back to Kunming. Surrounded by small but persistent Hani women, they try to bargain, but the prices (absurdly low by Western standards) have been fixed by the women, and they will only reduce them if they can sell several items at once.

Like all Hani, Long Mei is strictly honest, taking care to give the exact change. And, like the others, she can count in English and Japanese and can say a few words, like "beautiful apron, two for ten, beautiful bag, beautiful dress". When the tourists have gone, the Hani women sit in the sun and have an early lunch before the next group of buses arrives at midday. The new tourists set off for their afternoon trip through the Stone Forest, shepherded by a guide, who is often short-tempered with the swarms of Hani. Usually, Long Mei follows a group round the forest chanting "beautiful apron" until they succumb. Other women, particularly those with children strapped to their backs and their embroideries carried in a satchel, stay near the hotel gates rather than trek through the crowded forest waiting for the tourists to return, eventually, for their supper. Many tourists will spend up to £30 on embroidered goods and about half of that is profit for the Hani, after the cloth and ribbon has been paid for.

One of Long Mei's cousins, who has a very pretty voice, belongs to a dance troupe which gives a performance of Hani songs and dances every evening in the tourist hotel. Hani girls have high-pitched, sweet voices, and a local speciality is "leaf music", which is like a sophisticated (and more tuneful) version of the noise made by blowing through a blade of grass between your thumbs. The troupe is a new one, formed specially for the tourists when what had been a restaurant and guest house for locals expanded a few years ago to provide overnight accommodation for foreign tourists. This allowed the local Hani to increase their production of embroidery and participate in the economic boom that the tourists have brought about.

THE YOUNG PAINTER

Su Xuehua is 26 and a painter. She has just returned from two years studying in Paris on a Government scholarship. Her family is a cultured one, although both her parents are musicians, not painters. Her father is conductor of the local symphony orchestra and her mother composes music for films at

A disco in Xiamen, Fujian province. Condemned in the Cultural Revolution and more recently in the "Campaign against spiritual pollution", pop music and disco-dancing are immensely popular, and pirated cassette tapes of Hong Kong pop songs are widely sold.

the Shanghai Film Studio. Though their interests are different the house was always filled with books and pictures and many of her parents' friends are painters. She began painting before she went to school. A friend of her mother's used to teach her to paint with a Chinese brush and she won a few children's painting competitions when she was small. Later she started to go to art classes after school in the Children's Palace, and it was there she developed her love of oils.

Su Xuehua's parents suffered during the Cultural Revolution, when Western things were virtually banned. Both her parents spent many months in "cadre school" in the countryside, digging, hoeing, harvesting and looking after livestock as a corrective to their luxurious, Western-oriented way of life in Shanghai. Fortunately, they were usually sent separately, so Su Xuehua and her brother (who is now doing his Ph.D. in computer studies in America) were not left alone to fend for themselves. Her father taught his orchestra to play "patriotic" Chinese-composed music and only let them play Beethoven and Mozart in secret, just to keep in practice.

In 1976, when the Cultural Revolution was over, the orchestra began to play Tchaikovsky, Beethoven and Mozart at public concerts, which were always sold out. Su Xuehua began to paint in oils again and had no difficulty in getting into art school when she left school. She concentrated on oil painting and soon realized that she had to go abroad to study. The West is where oil painting developed and although she could

A student in Peking Arts School drawing from plaster casts of Western classical sculptures. Her jeans and tight T-shirt would have been considered improper during the Cultural Revolution.

look at the reproductions in art books she needed to see the real paintings in Western museums for herself.

Though she is very talented Su Xuehua knows that she probably owes her scholarship to her parents. Their connections in the art world, their old friends, helped her to get one of the very few scholarships for painters. Tens of thousands of young Chinese art students applied for two places abroad, and Su Xuehua was successful. If her parents had been peasants she would not have succeeded, no matter what her talent. She might have remained a name amongst thousands of others.

Su Xuehua mostly enjoyed her stay in Europe. She lived very simply, cooking for herself and walking everywhere to save money so that she could travel to see the museums in Italy, England and Germany. She found Europe very expensive and couldn't understand people's obsession with possessions. Su Xuehua spent her money on postcards of the paintings she saw in different museums and on film, to photograph the famous buildings and places she visited in Europe. She did not know if she would ever get the chance to come back so she had to try and remember everything.

When she first arrived in Europe she painted scenes from China's history, grand paintings of epic events which baffled her teachers in Paris. Under their influence, she began to paint in a softer, more impressionistic way, but she always painted figures and landscapes. She explains:

"In China, people don't understand abstract painting. We don't have the same traditions as in Europe. In the Cultural Revolution, people were put in prison for painting abstract paintings or simple landscapes. Then, we always had to show the glories of Communism. So, if you painted a beautiful landscape, you would paint in a few pylons to show that the Communist party had brought electricity to the remote mountain villages. Or else you would put a row of peasants into a painting of rice-fields, to show that peasants worked hard under socialism. It isn't the same now, we are freer to paint more or less what we like, but we are still supposed to teach people to improve themselves through our paintings. So I am still careful. If I paint pictures of Paris, I paint well-known buildings that people can recognize, or I paint people doing things: flower-sellers, vegetable markets, porters in the meat market, workers doing their work. That way, I don't think I will be criticized."

When she came back from Paris Su Xuehua was made a member of the Shanghai Artists' Association and she now works full-time as a painter. She receives a wage from the State and her paintings are sometimes commissioned for airport buildings, new hotels and government reception rooms. They are reproduced as covers for magazines and she has produced quite a few series of illustrations for books.

She is thinking of getting married but it is not easy.

"Men are afraid of clever wives and they don't want a wife who has been abroad. They think I've been affected by Western ways and that I won't be a docile housewife. A lot of my friends have the same problem. We know it isn't our fault. There are quite a lot of articles in the papers about the problems girls have in finding husbands. Men want obedient, stupid wives who they can dominate. People like me, from an intellectual background, with a good education and having studied abroad, nobody wants us."

Her parents have asked their friends to look for a husband for Su. Though she believes in free choice, and doesn't want an arranged marriage, she accepts that this may be the only way to meet a husband.

Su Xuehua's friends, painters like herself, poets, writers and musicians, are unlike many of the ordinary young people in China. They meet to discuss art and literature and talk late into the night. Quite a few of her friends are already divorced, which is unusual in China. Divorce is considered a disgrace and it is very difficult to marry a second time. The new one-child family policy is making it even more difficult, for both partners. If a woman has a child and meets an unmarried man his mother will oppose their marriage because she wants a grandchild of her own. A divorced man, even if he doesn't have custody of his child, may well find himself up against the same problem, because he and his new wife will not be allowed to have a child.

So, for Su Xuehua and her friends, their rather privileged position, their better education, their chances to go abroad, sometimes have negative effects on their life back in China.

GLOSSARY

acupuncture A technique whereby fine needles are inserted into different parts of the body to relieve pain. Acupuncture has been used in China for well over 2000 years. Its pain-relieving effects, which operate via the nervous system in a way that is still not fully understood, are now being studied throughout the world.

calligraphy For several thousand years the Chinese have been using soft brushes and ink to draw the thousands of different characters that make up their written language. A character may consist of over twenty separate brushstrokes and it is important to learn to "write" them in the proper order. Because of the beauty of the brush-strokes and the significance of the words, calligraphy has always been valued in China and is often more highly esteemed than painting.

Chiang Kai-shek and the Nationalists In 1911 the last imperial ruler was overthrown and the Republic of China established. Although the Nationalist Party was nominally in charge, many of the regional armies set up at the end of the 19th century were not disbanded and their leaders (known as "warlords") actually controlled many parts of China. In 1926 a young soldier called Chiang Kai-shek became leader of the Nationalists and tried to suppress both the warlords and the newly-formed Communist Party. When the Japanese invaded China in 1937, Chiang Kai-shek gradually retreated to the west of China. Meanwhile, the Communist Party, harassed all the time by Nationalist forces, began to be seen as the main body of resistance against the Japanese invasion. When Japan was defeated at the end of the Second World War, Chiang and the Communists fought a civil war for control of China. When Mao and the Communist Party finally won in 1949, the Nationalists moved to Taiwan.

Communist Party The Chinese Communist Party was founded in Shanghai in 1921. At first an underground organization, it later succeeded in driving out Chiang Kai-shek's Nationalist government in 1949. Though only about four per cent of the population belong to the Party, it is still the leading force within the Chinese government. The Party split away from the Soviet Union in 1960, when Mao disobeyed Russian practice by concentrating on agricultural reform rather than industrial progress. The Chinese Communist Party offered a different path for agricultural countries with underdeveloped industries.

Cultural Revolution Begun in 1966, the Cultural Revolution ended with Mao's death in 1976. It was started as a 'clean-up' of the Communist Party which Mao saw as corrupt; he unleashed young people in a campaign against their self-satisfied elders. Growing into a persecution campaign, the Cultural Revolution is now regarded as a disaster which seriously damaged China's international credibility as a stable nation.

Confucius An unsuccessful teacher who lived in the 5th and 4th centuries B.C., Confucius's ideas were taken up in the Han dynasty (206 B.C. to A.D. 220) and formed the basis of the imperial system of government which relied upon social stability and obedience.

Deng Xiaoping Born in 1904, Deng joined the Communist Party in 1924 and held a series of political and military posts until 1949. He was a top-ranking member of the Government from 1952

	until he was disgraced in the Cultural Revolution. Since 1976 and the death of Mao he has been recognized as the key figure in the Chinese leadership although he has relinquished many posts because of his age. He is still Chairman of the Communist Party Central Military Commission and the Central Advisory Commission.
Gang of Four	A radical faction within the Chinese Communist Party that emerged as a political force in the spring of 1976 and was suppressed later that year.
Japanese-Chinese relations	Because of the Japanese invasion of China in 1937 and the brutality of the Japanese soldiers, many Chinese still find it hard to accept the many Japanese businessmen in China. Despite recent history, Japan and China are close because Japan needs Chinese raw materials and China needs Japan's technological expertise. The relationship remains uneasy, however, for the Chinese resent the way the Japanese "dump" poor quality or out-of-date goods on the Chinese market, as well as the way they refuse to acknowledge their guilt for certain war crimes.
Mao Zedong	Born in 1893, Mao was radicalized very early by the poverty and decay he saw around him during the last years of the Qing dynasty (1644-1911). A founding member of the Chinese Communist Party, he fought several bitter power struggles to become its leader and his determination helped the Party to resist the Japanese and eventually take control of China in 1949. He was a less successful peace-time leader, prone to putting wild theories into practice and unleashing disastrous mass movements like the Cultural Revolution. He died in 1976.
minorities	Many non-Chinese people live in China, mostly on its borders. Some of the most important groups are Tibetan, Mongolian, Uighur and Kazakh, the last two being Moslem minorities who live in Chinese Central Asia, near the Russian border. Partly because they often live in sensitive border areas, their different languages and cultures are now promoted by the Chinese government and most are exempt from the one-child family restrictions. Minorities make up about six per cent of the total population.
peasants	Term used both traditionally and in modern times for all those Chinese who make a living from agriculture in the countryside.
Qin shi huang di	Emperor of the Qin dynasty, 221-207 B.C., he is often called China's first emperor. He led his armies to conquer all the other small separate states that arose when the central rule of the Zhou dynasty disintegrated (in about 700 B.C.). He is best known in China for his attempt to destroy the influence of Confucius by burning all the Confucian books he could find. Outside China he is better known for his "buried army". Before his death, like all Chinese he had planned his burial. A huge mound was built, filled with precious objects and maps of the sky and seas, with mercury running along the river courses. On all sides of the mound, huge pits were dug and filled with several thousand larger-than-life soldiers and horses made of baked clay. These "armies" were intended to defend the tomb against evil spirits. They were first unearthed in the 1970s by peasants digging a well. Now, several thousand of the figures have been restored and the "buried army" is perhaps the most popular tourist site in China.

BOOK LIST

BOOKS FOR YOUNGER READERS

Loescher, Gil and Ann — *China: pushing toward the year 2000*, Harcourt, Brace, Jovanovich, 1981

Merton, Anna and Kan, Shio-yun — *China: the land and its people*, Macdonald, 1986

Money, D.C. — *China: the land and the people*, Evans Brothers, 1984

Tames, Richard — *China Today*, Kaye and Ward, 1978

Yuan-ming, Shui and Thompson, Stuart — *Chinese Stories*, Wayland, 1986

Wood, Frances — *Through the Year in China*, Batsford, 1981

BOOKS FOR OLDER READERS AND FOR REFERENCE

Gray, Jack and White, Gordan (eds.) — *China's New Development Strategy*, Academic Press, 1982

Hooper, Beverley — *Youth in China*, Penguin, 1986

Houying, Dai — *The Stones of the Wall*, Michael Joseph, 1985

Jie, Zhang — *Leaden Wings*, Virago, 1987

Pan, Lynn — *The New Chinese Revolution*, Hamish Hamilton, 1987

Wilson, Dick — *Mao: the people's emperor*, Futura, 1980

(*Leaden Wings* and *The Stones of the Wall* are novels translated from Chinese; Zhang Jie describes aspects of industrial reform and Dai Houying, the lingering effect of the Cultural Revolution.)

ACKNOWLEDGMENTS

The Author and Publishers would like to thank Sally and Richard Greenhill for the photographs on pages 4, 8, 12 (bottom), 13, 15, 16, 17, 19, 20 (top), 23 (bottom), 24, 25, 29, 30, 31, 34, 36, 37, 42, 46 (top), 47 (middle), 48, 50, 52, 58 and 59. The remaining photographs were taken by the author. The map on page 3 was drawn by R.F. Brien.

INDEX

agriculture 4, 10-17
air transport 5, 37-8
armed forces 9, 11

bicycles 21, 25, 29, 33, 41, 45-7
boats 48-50
Buddhism (see religion)
Buried Army (see Xi'an)
buses 47, 50-5

Chiang Kai-shek 11
children 24, 30, 35
Christianity (see religion)
clothes 9, 14-15, 17, 36-7, 39, 44, 59
communes 12
Communist Party 3, 7, 26, 27, 44, 59
Confucius 6, 27
Confucianism (see religion)
crafts 55-7
crime 29
Cultural Revolution 7, 9, 19, 27-9, 32, 35, 54-5, 58-9

dance 55, 57-8
Deng Xiaoping 7
divorce 28, 60

education 27-9, 33-5
export 6, 22-3, 28

fish 5, 12, 15
food 9, 15-17, 21, 32, 34, 39, 44, 46, 53
foot-binding 6

Government 7, 9, 11-15, 18-19, 22, 24, 27, 37, 39
Grand Canal 45
Great Wall 3, 40

holidays 15, 20
Hong Kong 14, 16, 37, 42, 58
housing 13, 21, 24-6, 33, 41-2, 53

industry 5, 18-26
irrigation 3, 4, 12-13
Islam (see religion)

Japanese 5, 11, 13, 18-19, 33, 37, 38, 39, 41, 42, 45, 50, 52

law 28-30
leisure 30, 34, 38, 43

management 8, 18-19, 20, 22
Mao Zedong 3, 7, 11, 22, 28
markets 14, 29, 36, 44, 50, 55
marriage 26, 28, 41, 53, 60
medicine 16, 26, 30-3, 39
mining 24-6
minorities 56-7
music 43, 54, 57, 58

opera 54
one-child family policy (see population)

Painting 23, 34, 58-60
Peking 10-11, 28-30, 33, 38, 45, 48, 50-3, 55

population 8, 10, 14, 24, 26, 30, 56

railways 4, 38, 45-6
religion 6, 7, 16, 39
retirement 9, 24, 26, 42, 43
roads 4, 27, 50-3

Shanghai 11, 18, 22, 38, 40-2, 43, 46, 48, 55, 58
shops 36-7
silk 11, 20, 22, 39
Soviet Union 7, 18, 54

Taoism (see religion)
tax 12, 13, 39
taxis 51-3
television 21, 26, 29, 33, 35
textiles 6, 20-4
timber 4
tourism 5, 16, 22, 24, 37-40, 46, 49, 52, 56-7
transport 4, 16, 45-53

unemployment 8, 24-5, 43-4

wages 18, 21, 23-5, 27-8, 32-3, 42, 51-5
women 6, 26

Xi'an 5, 38, 39, 40